ONE WORLD BOOKS

LIVING TOGETHER

EDITED BY

RHODRI JONES

HEINEMANN EDUCATIONAL BOOKS

Other titles in the One World series

Growing Up
One World Poets
Moving On

Cover illustrations Teri Gower

Heinemann Educational Books Ltd
22 Bedford Square, London WC1B 3HH

LONDON EDINBURGH MELBOURNE AUCKLAND
SINGAPORE KUALA LUMPUR
NEW DELHI IBADAN NAIROBI JOHANNESBURG
PORTSMOUTH (NH) KINGSTON

First published 1986

ISBN 0 435 10469 1

Typeset by Fakenham Photosetting Ltd, Fakenham, Norfolk
Printed and bound in Great Britain by Richard Clay (The Chaucer Press), Bungay, Suffolk

CONTENTS

INTRODUCTION: ONE WORLD BOOKS

The English language has not one but many forms. It is spoken with many different accents: for instance, Scots, Midlands, Northern, West Country, Cockney, Jamaican, Trinidadian, Nigerian, Australian. The list could be made much longer and readers can no doubt think of other accents to add to the list. People from different regions often use their own special words, with which other speakers of English may not be familiar. For instance, someone from north-east Scotland might ask a person to 'Dicht the table wi' a clout', or say that he or she was feeling 'wabbit', and a speaker from south-east England might be mystified as to the meaning. Alternatively, a northerner might not know the meaning of 'gimp' or a 'git'. There are other words such as 'billabong', 'boogoo', 'breeks', 'braw', 'akee' and 'takkies' which are known and used by English-speakers in some parts of the world and not in others. There are many, many more words and no doubt readers could extend the list themselves very easily.

What does this range and diversity of accent, vocabulary and usage mean? Does it mean that the English language is 'in decay', 'falling to bits', 'slipping'? Certainly not. The range and diversity of the English language are not new. They existed in the time of Chaucer, Shakespeare and Dr Samuel Johnson. Twentieth-century writers such as D. H. Lawrence (in a poem such as 'The Collier's Wife') and James Kirkup (in his autobiographical *The Only Child*) have shown how regional accents and vocabulary persisted in Nottingham and South Shields in their boyhoods. We should see this range and diversity as part of the richness of English, and they are particularly noticeable in spoken English. Because literature is about the way people think, feel and communicate with each other, good writing can convey very vividly the different rhythms of speech and the range of the spoken word. Many of the extracts and poems in this series of anthologies demonstrate just how diverse, and how satisfying, the range of spoken and written English can be.

A key feature of the English language, along with other world languages such as French, Spanish and Arabic, is that it is spoken and written by people of many races and many cultures. In many cases, as with the spread of French and Spanish, English was used as the language of government in far-flung parts of the British Empire. Consequently it began to be spoken and written by people in regions as far apart as the Indian sub-continent and the West African Gold Coast, and on islands as distant from each other as Ceylon and Barbados. English was also taken far beyond the shores of our island by settlers seeking their fortunes and a better life in Canada, Australia, New Zealand, South Africa and, earliest of all, North America. So English is a very widely used and a very cosmopolitan language. It is used for business, for government, for education, for news coverage, for everyday communication, and it is used by writers of poetry, prose and drama in an enormous number of countries scattered around the world. Most of these countries were once

British colonies and are now members of the Commonwealth of Nations.

This series of anthologies aims to bring into British classrooms the diverse voices and 'melodies' of English from the work of a wide range of English-speaking writers. Some of them live on this island, and others speak and write in English but do not call England 'home'.

There is another very important group of writers whose work is represented in these pages. These are men and women from, in the main, the Caribbean, Africa and the Indian sub-continent who have now settled in Britain. Their contribution is often distinctive and original and their view of British life is frequently from the position of an outsider or newcomer. Their work tends to reflect particular concerns: the themes of exile and the search for identity in a new, often hostile and discriminatory, society are prominent. In some instances they draw on their experiences before coming to Britain. Their language, too, often reflects the rhythms and special vocabularies of their former homes.

Certainly the range of writing now available to English-speakers and readers of English is exciting and challenging. These anthologies are intended to make the full range of writing in English accessible to British pupils. By doing so they aim to make a strong contribution to the multi-cultural curriculum. If we can only listen to these diverse voices, tuning the English language to their own distinctive use, we will surely understand ourselves and the world so much better.

INTRODUCTION: LIVING TOGETHER

It may still be argued by some people that the television play is not an art form. What cannot be disputed is that more people are likely to see a play on television than would ever see it in the theatre. It is sobering to reflect that the audience watching a play by Shakespeare on television (not the same as a television play) is probably larger than the total of all those seeing it in the many productions there have been in the theatre since the play was first written four hundred or so years ago. For that reason if for no other, television plays deserve to be studied. Television can speak so immediately to its audience and with such impact that it is important to be able to understand the techniques being used and to be able to discriminate between what is good and what is mediocre, between what is honest and what is manipulative.

Inevitably there is a difference between viewing a play on television with all its artistic aids of actors, setting, music, lighting and so on, and simply reading the words on the page. The effect of the latter is bound to be less. But it does allow the imagination to be brought into play, and it enables the intentions and skill of the writer to be more closely studied.

Techniques of television can be examined for their effectiveness – the use of voice-over, the use of vision without words, the cutting from one scene to another, the economy with which dramatic points are made, the use of close-ups, the use of the camera to represent the point of view of a particular character. But even without this, the narrative, the characters, the writer's intentions can all emerge from the bare words of the original script.

The four plays selected here represent different types of television drama. *The Street Party* and *Royston's Day* are two episodes from the situation comedy *Empire Road*. *The Evacuees* is a play conceived and written for television. *A Chip of Glass Ruby* is a television adaptation and expansion by the author of her own short story.

The writers come from different backgrounds – Michael Abbensetts was born in Guyana, Jack Rosenthal comes of a Jewish family, Nadine Gordimer was born in South Africa – but all the plays show a concern for people and the problem of living together. There are the tensions and affections of family life. There are the conflicts and misunderstandings of race and religion.

The Street Party and *Royston's Day* approach the theme of living together from the point of view of comedy and the intention to entertain in a kind of black *Coronation Street*. *The Street Party* introduces the reader to the strongly drawn characters who live in Empire Road. We see the slick, strong-willed and dominating Everton, his flashy and snobbish wife, Hortense, and their son, Marcus, who sees things his way and has his own views about integration – particularly when this involves the lovely Ranjanaa. There is also Miss May, struggling determinedly against unequal economic odds, and trying to cope with the Rastafarian stances of her sons Desmond and Royston. *The Street Party* highlights the different viewpoints of black and Asian parents and their children, and presents, in a witty and highly perceptive way, the black British experience of multi-racial Britain.

Royston's Day uses the same frame of situation comedy to explore the themes of racism, marriage and work in the lives of the key characters of Empire Road. Desmond and Royston react with characteristic vigour when a white night-club manager bars them from his club. Even the successful Everton finds that racism bars him as well, when he tries to enter the same premises in an effort to prove or disprove Royston's story that he was discriminated against because he was black. Marcus and Ranjanaa decide to override their parents' prejudices because of their love for each other, and Walter and Miss May take the plunge – a move which seems to benefit Miss May more than the meek and nervous Walter. Finally, Desmond and Royston make different decisions about 'Babylon' and the world of work.

Jack Rosenthal's play *The Evacuees* focuses on two young working-class Jewish boys and their family during the Second World War. They try to cope with their changed living conditions when they are evacuated to the relative safety of Blackpool from Manchester. Their new foster mother is cold and harsh but they endure stoically for as long as they can. The bleak, middle-class, childless foster home provided by Mr and Mrs Graham is contrasted with the warmth and vigour of the boys' own Jewish family life to which they eventually return.

Nadine Gordimer's play *A Chip of Glass Ruby* takes a hard but compassionate look at the lives of those who live under 'apartheid' and who try to defy its laws. She depicts the unglamorous and courageous Indian mother and wife, Mrs Bamjee, who braves the South African police, and her husband's disapproval, as she joins other Indians and Africans in their fight against enforced removals and inferior schooling.

Each of these plays, in its distinctive way, provides a rich and varied commentary on family life and on individuals responding in different ways to a range of social and political situations. In their different ways each one extends our understanding of human nature.

ACKNOWLEDGEMENTS

The publishers would like to thank the following for permission to reproduce copyright material:

Blake Friedmann Literary, TV and Film Agency, 42 Bloomsbury Street, London WC1B 3QJ, for *The Street Party* and *Royston's Day*, two episodes from *Empire Road* by Michael Abbensetts.

Margaret Ramsay Ltd, 14A Goodwin's Court, St Martin's Lane, London WC2N 4LL, for *The Evacuees* by Jack Rosenthal.

A. P. Watt Ltd, 26–28 Bedford Row, London WC1R 4HL, for *A Chip of Glass Ruby* by Nadine Gordimer.

Illustrations were provided by the following:

Mark Urgent, page 1; John Morris, page 41; Emily Booth, page 94.

The photograph on page 95 from *A Chip of Glass Ruby* was supplied by courtesy of the distributors, Telepool.

Michael Abbensetts

Michael Abbensetts was born in Guyana in 1938. He was educated there and in Canada, and came to England in 1963. He has been Visiting Playwright and Playwright-in-Residence at the Carnegie–Mellon University in the USA and has written plays for the theatre, television and radio. Among his stage plays are *Sweet Talk*, *Alterations*, *Samba*, *In the Mood*, *Outlaw* and *El Dorado*. As well as writing two series of *Empire Road*, his plays for television include *The Museum Attendant*, *Inner City Blues*, *Crime and Passion*, *Black Christmas*, *Roadrunner* and *Easy Money*. *Empire Road* has also been published as a novel.

Empire Road deals with a group of characters, mainly black, who live in a particular area of Birmingham. In some ways, it attempts to create a kind of black equivalent of *Coronation Street*. But *Empire Road* is a situation comedy (or sit com) whereas *Coronation Street* is soap opera.

A sit com, as its name suggests, is a comedy arising out of a particular situation. The main characters tend to reappear in each episode, and the comedy and interest lie in seeing how they respond to each new situation. Certain story-lines and interplays of character develop from episode to episode, but generally each episode has a completeness about it and can be taken on its own.

With soap opera there is less sense of completeness about each episode. There may be humorous interludes, but the main emphasis is on dramatic and emotional happenings. Episodes end in suspense with cliff-hangers to make the viewer want to watch next time to find out what happens. Soap opera tries to give the effect that you are watching 'real life' and that the characters actually exist off the screen as well as on. In a sense, soap opera rejects 'completeness'. It just goes on and on and on – like life. *Coronation Street, Crossroads* and *The Archers*, for instance, have been running for years.

The Street Party was the first episode in the first series of *Empire Road*.

EMPIRE ROAD

THE STREET PARTY

CHARACTERS

EVERTON BENNETT
HORTENSE BENNETT
MARCUS BENNETT
WALTER
MAY
DESMOND
ROYSTON
KATE MORRIS
RANJANAA
MR KAPOOR
LINDA
CUSTOMERS

Scene 1
Ext. Soho Road. Day.

> *We open on taxi going down Soho Road. Continuing theme song. We establish* EVERTON, HORTENSE *and* MARCUS *inside.*

Scene 2
Int. No. 72 Empire Road. Kitchen. Day.

> MRS MAY REID *is in her kitchen. A plump West Indian woman. A woman who always struggles to make ends meet. Skirt, cardigan mismatched. She is making a pot of pig-tail soup. She samples it with a spoon. Someone knocks at back door. It is* WALTER ISAACS. *She goes to door. Does not open immediately.*

MISS MAY: Who?
WALTER (*off*):   Wa-Wa-Walter Isaacs.

> *She opens back door.* WALTER ISAACS *enters. West Indian. Forties. Glasses. Stutters. Abrupt, nervous laugh.*

WALTER: Afternoon.
MISS MAY (*interrupting*):   Ah might as well tell yuh now, ah ain' got it!
WALTER: Doan s-say dat, Miss M-May.

> *He is looking at the soup.*

MISS MAY: It's pig-tail soup. Yuh want some?
WALTER: N-No . . . no.
MISS MAY: Force yuhself. Go on.
WALTER (*trying not to succumb*):   Ah c-came about odder things.
MISS MAY: Have some soup firse.
WALTER: De r-rent, Miss May.
MISS MAY: Forget it. Have some pig-tail soup instead.
WALTER (*loud for him*):   De rent, please!
MISS MAY: Here. Who you shoutin' at? Doan shout at me in my own kitchen.
WALTER: Sorry, but it's due t-today. Yuh r-rent.
MISS MAY: Nex' week. Ah'll have it nex' week.
WALTER: Today.
MISS MAY: Yuh doan understan' *Heng-lish*. Ah can't pay yuh till nex' week.
WALTER: B-but he's c-comin' ba-ba-back *today*.
MISS MAY: Who dat?
WALTER: De boss. 'E's comin' b-back today.
MISS MAY: Bennett? Bennett de landlord comin' back today?
WALTER: If ah doan have dat rent 'e'll kill me.

> MISS MAY *holds back door open for him to go.*

MISS MAY: Rubbish. He's married to yuh sister.

WALTER (*abrupt laugh*):   Yes, an' 'e blames me fo' dat as well.

Scene 3

Ext. Empire Road. Day.

>   EVERTON *meanwhile spots some flags and posters announcing a forthcoming event in the street.*

EVERTON: Flags. Reckon dey know I'm back? Preparing a big welcome for me.

MARCUS: A lynchin' perhaps?

Scene 4

Ext/Int. EVERTON's *front door and hallway.*

>   *We hear front door bell being rung.* WALTER *hurries to answer door. He opens front door to* EVERTON, HORTENSE *and* MARCUS, *who walk past him.*

WALTER: W-w- ... Wel-wel ...

>   EVERTON *steers him out of way.*

EVERTON: Yes, yes, we know, Walter. (WALTER *at a loss*) Doan jus' stan' dere, Walter.

MARCUS: Hello, banner.[1]

WALTER: Am, hello, M-Marcus.

HORTENSE (*to* EVERTON):   He was tryin' to say 'welcome'.

EVERTON: Woman, it takes yuh brodder twenty minutes to say what it takes normal people twenty seconds.

HORTENSE: Everton, stop dat.

>   WALTER, *cornered, laughs.*

EVERTON: Hasn't changed a bit, has 'e? (*To* WALTER) Ah'm talkin' about you, Mr Hyena.

WALTER: W-w-w-wel ... wel ...

Scene 5

Int. The BENNETTS' *kitchen. Day.*

>   *Quite a large kitchen.* EVERTON *sitting down at kitchen table.* WALTER *as well.* HORTENSE *making pot of tea.*

---

[1] *banner*: good friend, partner. The author says, 'I only added the term to Marcus because the actor playing him was intrigued by the word and was always using it.'

EVERTON: Hortense. Ah dyin' fo' a cup of tea.

HORTENSE: What yuh think ah'm doin' wit' dis tea-pot?

EVERTON: Ah dunno. If it was a cow ah'd say yuh was milkin' it.

He laughs. Not too loudly. People who own property do not laugh too loudly.

WALTER: So how was G-G-G ...?

EVERTON: G-G-G? What's G-G-G?

WALTER (*struggling for the word*):   Guyana ...!

EVERTON (*amused, wiping his face as* WALTER *spits as well*):   Lord, ah hope yuh provide a towel wit' yuh showers.

HORTENSE: Everton!

EVERTON: Yuh brodder's practisin' to be a punk rocker.

WALTER: How was it? G-Guyana?

EVERTON: Yuh wouldn't recognize de place.

HORTENSE: Dat's not true, Walter.

EVERTON: Doan worry wit' her, Walter. De place has changed completely. Ah was glad to rush back to Englan'.

HORTENSE: Well, Guyana is still my home.

EVERTON: Home? What home? Englan' is yuh home now, woman. So, Walter ... yuh had any trouble since we bin away?

WALTER: Well, ah had a b-bit uh trouble, h-here ... (*He rises and indicates his back, a back injury.*)

EVERTON: Is dis man sane? Business troubles, Walter, not back troubles! My shop an' my houses.

WALTER: Oh! (*He laughs his nervous laugh.*)

EVERTON: Oh, rant,[2] oh, rant. Ah've only bin back five minutes an' already ah'm headin' for a nervous breakdown. (*Then*) What about de rents? Ah hope yuh got everybody's rent up to date.

WALTER: Well ...

EVERTON: 'Well'? A well is a thing dey dig in de groun' fo' *water*. Ah'm talkin' about money, not water. Look, tell me calmly before ah burst a blood vessel. When ah went away ah left you in charge of four houses. Yuh haven't sold dem by any chance, have you? Ah mean, ah still own four houses, don't I?

WALTER (*cornered laugh*):   What! What! Course yuh do. Always jokin', aren't you?

EVERTON: Jokin'? Jokin'? God give me strength. (*He rises.*) Okay, okay. Tell yuh what. Ah'll go an' see fo' m'self.

WALTER: Now?

EVERTON: Why not? Gimme de keys, some uh dem might be at work.

WALTER: B-but yuh only jus' arrive.

EVERTON: So? Dey's my properties, ain' dey? I's de landlord. Ah'll go an' say

---

[2] *Oh, rant*: a cleaned-up version of a West Indian swearword.

hello. (*To* HORTENSE) Ah'll see yuh later.

WALTER: What about de s-shop?

EVERTON: Dat can wait till tomorrow.

EVERTON *goes*.

HORTENSE: Do you want a biscuit, Walter?

WALTER (*unhearing, still staring after* EVERTON):   Eh?

MARCUS *enters. Still in Afghan waistcoat.*

MARCUS: So, how're things, banner?

HORTENSE: Marcus, doan start dat again.

MARCUS (*so innocently*):   Start what, Mother?

HORTENSE: Callin' everyone 'banner'. He's your uncle, show him some re-spect.

MARCUS: Okay. How're things, Uncle Banner?

HORTENSE: Marcus!

Scene 6

Ext. Front door. No. 72 Empire Road. Day.

We see EVERTON *ringing doorbell of No. 72. He waits, no response. He produces his own keys. Decides against using them and goes around the back.*

Scene 7

Ext. Back door. No. 72 Empire Road. Day.

We see EVERTON *approaching back door. It is ajar. Reggae guitars can be heard.* EVERTON *knocks.*

Scene 8

Int. MAY's *front room. Day.*

DESMOND *and* ROYSTON *dancing.*

Scene 9

Int. MAY's *kitchen. Day.*

EVERTON: Hello. Anybody home?

Scene 10

Int. MAY's *front room. Day.*

EVERTON *follows sound of music to front room. Door is open. Sees two Rastafarian[3] youths dancing.*

EVERTON: Oh God ...! (*They don't hear him.*) What de hell yo-all doin'?
DESMOND: Who the rahtid[4] are you?
EVERTON: What you two doin' in my house!
DESMOND: Your house? Your house?

Scene 11
Int. HORTENSE *and* EVERTON*'s stairs and hallway. Day.*

WALTER: G-guess what? They're havin' a street p-party.
HORTENSE (*suspiciously*):   Oh so that's what all those flags were about.
EVERTON (*off*):   Walter! Walter! Where is 'e?
WALTER: Oh, God. Ah k-knew it.
EVERTON (*off*):   Where is dat stutterin' fool!
HORTENSE: He's up here.
EVERTON (*off*):   Jigaboos![5] Jigaboos!

EVERTON *comes charging in.*

EVERTON: You know what 'e's done! You know what dis *brodder* of yours has done?
HORTENSE: Not so loud, Everton.
EVERTON: Are you listenin' to me, woman!
HORTENSE (*mildly*):   Yes, yes.
EVERTON: He's got rid of all my best people. An' put in a load of strangers instead. Asians! Walter's rented one of my houses to an Asian family! You should see what dey done to dat front room. Dey turned it into a mosque.
WALTER: A temple.[6]
EVERTON: Temple, mosque,[7] it's all de same to me. Dey pray in dere now.
HORTENSE: Walter, say it's not so.
WALTER: A-a-a- ...

He is ignored.

EVERTON: Dey's worse.
HORTENSE: Worse?
EVERTON: He's got a bunch of Rastafarians livin' at number seventy-two.

---

[3] *Rastafarian*: member of a religious cult that originated in Jamaica and believes in the divinity of Haile Selasse, the former Emperor of Ethiopia.
[4] *rahtid*: another cleaned-up version of the swearword 'rant'. It is used by Jamaicans.
[5] *Jigaboo*: Wild man. A term of abuse a black man might use against another black.
[6] *temple*: Hindu place of worship.
[7] *mosque*: Muslim place of worship.

HORTENSE: Yuh mean like in Shanty Town[8] in Jamaica?

WALTER (*funny to him*):   No, man, dey're ...!

EVERTON: Fool, it's not funny! ...

WALTER: Dey're not real R-R-Rass-ta-farians.

EVERTON: Well, they got plaited hair, haven't they, and the caps? In my book dat makes dem Rastafarians! Jigaboos!

WALTER: Dey're o-out of w-work.

EVERTON: Yuh hear dat! He's rented my property to people who're out of work. Oh, God. Make an appointment for me to see my doctor. Ah'm gonna be sick, ah know it. My own brodder-in-law. What did ah do to him? Tell me. Tell me. Six months. Ah jus' go away fo' six months an' in dat short, short, short time de man runs riot. Riot. Your brodder makes Judas Iscariot seem like a friend-in-need.

Pause.

Scene 12

Ext. Street outside school playground. Day.

We see MARCUS *passing by on the street outside school playground. A football comes flying over.* MARCUS *retrieves football. Throws it back over. We see the school playground, the young people playing, Asian, West Indian, English.*

KATE *calls to* MARCUS. *Walks towards him.* MARCUS *meets her half-way.*

MARCUS: Hello, Miss Morris.

KATE: Hello, Marcus. Stranger. Must be three years. I'm glad I saw you. I'm looking for volunteers. Do you have a minute?

MARCUS (*looking at his watch, great production*):   Volunteers? Well, not exactly...

An attractive young Asian woman joins them. RANJANAA (RANJU) KAPOOR. *The girl is striking. About eighteen.* MARCUS *can't take his eyes off her.*

KATE: Marcus, meet Ranju Kapoor. Marcus Bennett.

MARCUS: Hello.

RANJU (*made shy*):   Hello.

MARCUS: On second thoughts, Miss Morris, I can spare a minute or two. Or more.

KATE (*smiling, well aware of what's going on*):   I bet you can. Anyway, it's about the street parties. Have you heard about them?

We see MARCUS *is looking at* RANJANAA.

KATE: We're doing a number of parties in Thornley. Those Jubilee street

---

[8] *Shanty Town*: slum area.

parties went down so well, we thought we'd do a few more this year. We're going to do one in Empire Road. (*Cheerfully*) Which is asking for trouble, isn't it? Look, I'd better come right out and say it. I need all the help I can get on Saturday. You do want to help us, don't you? Course you do. (*She smiles*) Especially as Ranjanaa is going to be helping out as well.

RANJANAA: Miss Morris ...!

MARCUS (*still looking at* RANJANAA): Miss Morris, you've made me an offer ah can't refuse.

Scene 13

Int. MISS MAY's *fish and chip shop. Day.*

MISS MAY *behind counter. Her two sons* DESMOND *and* ROYSTON *drift in.*

MISS MAY: Good. Yuh jus' in time.

DESMOND *starts to leave.*

DESMOND: G'bye.

MISS MAY: Desmond! (DESMOND *returns, sucking his teeth.*) Hold on here fo' me. Ah got to go an' buy some yams an' sweet potatoes. (DESMOND *sucks his teeth again.*) An' doan suck yuh teeth at me, boy. Now, get behin' here.

DESMOND *and* ROYSTON *go behind counter.* MISS MAY *ties a scarf on her head and is leaving.*

DESMOND: Doan take all day. (*She goes. Pause.* DESMOND *turns happily to his brother.*) Chips, buddy. Chips, fadder!

They help themselves to chips like naughty little boys. LINDA CATER *enters. English, twenties, chewing gum.*

DESMOND (*nudging* ROYSTON): Hey, Royston, ah dunno 'bout you but I could do wit' more dan jus' chips. As Jah[9] 'imself said: man shall not live by chips alone.

ROYSTON *gives a snorting laugh.* LINDA *makes a face.*

LINDA: Cod 'n' chips, twice ... (*a beat*) Please.

DESMOND: I an' I[10] can deliver dem, if yuh want.

Another snorting laugh from ROYSTON. MARCUS *enters.*

MARCUS: Linda?

LINDA: Marcus! Didn't know you were back.

MARCUS: Three cod 'n' chips.

---

[9] *Jah*: the Rastafarian word for 'Lord', 'God'.
[10] *I an' I*: the Rastafarian way of saying 'we'.

DESMOND: I only got one han'. (*To her*) Vinegar?

LINDA (*to* MARCUS):   How come you haven't phoned my sister?

MARCUS: Cos your father wouldn't like it, dat's why.

LINDA: Oh him.

DESMOND: Royston, how come you let dis man chat up your girl like dat?

ROYSTON: *My* girl?

DESMOND: Well, she can't be my girl. No man but me would dare chat up my girl.

LINDA: Why don't you two grow up, eh? I'll tell your mother.

DESMOND: Who de rathid care you tell?

MARCUS: Hey, none uh that. She's a customer. It's *you* who need her.

DESMOND: Royston . . . man here lookin' for trouble. Him mus' know karate.

> ROYSTON *snarls at* MARCUS.

MARCUS: Banner, ah hope you're capable of murder. Because I am. Yuh understand what I'm telling you? You better think about dat before you come across dat counter.

DESMOND: Cool it, cool it.

MARCUS: Now give Linda her cod an' stop makin' waves. (DESMOND *serves* LINDA.) Come on, let's go, Linda. Fish 'n' chips is not my favourite food, anyway.

> MARCUS *and* LINDA *leave shop.*

Scene 14

Ext. Chip shop. Day.

LINDA: Boys tryin' to be men.

> *We see* RANJANAA *passing by on the other side of the road.* MARCUS *spots her.*

MARCUS: Listen, ah'll see yuh. Ranju! Excuse me, Linda.

> *He crosses street to join* RANJANAA.

LINDA: Charming.

Scene 15

Ext. Empire Road.

> *We see* MARCUS *as he catches up with* RANJANAA.

MARCUS: Hello. Don't look now but you're being followed.

RANJANAA: You must not shout my name like that. Not on the street. Please.

MARCUS: I was hopin' ah'd see you again.

RANJANAA: What for?

MARCUS: Ah like to get to know my neighbours.
RANJANAA: That girl, is she one of your neighbours too?
MARCUS: Girl? What girl?
RANJANAA: I bet you know a number of girls.
MARCUS: A number of girls? No, never. A *lot* yes, sure. But a number, no. (RANJANAA *gives him a look*.) Ranju, ah was hopin' ah'd see you again. Ah want to take you out. Can I?

There is an Indian sweet shop at the corner of the street.

RANJANAA: Maybe. Maybe not. Now, there is my father's shop. I work there. Do not follow me any more, please.

She starts to cross the road.

MARCUS: Will I see you again?

She walks away. Enters sweet shop. He is just left standing there.

Scene 16
Int. EVERTON's *food store. Day.*

MISS MAY *in the shop.* EVERTON *near the till.*

MISS MAY: Yuh got any yams, Mistah Man?
EVERTON: Lady, my name is not 'Mister Man'. Yes, ah got yams. Can't yuh see dem? De shop full uh yams.
MISS MAY: Ah'm sorry ah asked.
EVERTON: I know you, you're Miss May, ain' yuh?
MISS MAY: Yes, man, ah'm livin' in one uh yuh houses now.
EVERTON: So you're Miss May.
MISS MAY: Ah believe yuh met m'two sons Desmon' an' Royston.
EVERTON: Doan remind me.
MISS MAY: Dey's two good boys.
EVERTON: Dey said de same about Frank an' Jesse James.
MISS MAY: It's de house ah want to talk to you about.
EVERTON: What's wrong wit' de house? Nothing wrong wit' dat house.
MISS MAY: It's a bit damp.
EVERTON: Damp? Naw. No way. Damp?
MISS MAY: Mistuh Man, every night ah got to go to sleep wit' an um-brella!
EVERTON: Every man to 'is own taste. Some people prefer to sleep wit' a blanket. (*He laughs happily.*)
MISS MAY: Ah'm glad you t'ink it's funny.
EVERTON: How about de rent, Miss May? Ah doan think dat's funny.
MISS MAY: Ah haven't forgotten.
EVERTON: Believe me, Miss May, ah wouldn't let yuh forget.
MISS MAY: Ah'll pay you T'ursday.

EVERTON: Ah see.

MISS MAY: Yuh doan believe me?

EVERTON: Miss May, ah've bin a lan'lord fo' a long, long time. Dat doan make it easy fo' me to have much faith in human nature. But ah tell yuh what. In your case ah'm prepared to make an exception. Yuh got until Friday mornin'.

MISS MAY: Mistuh Man, yuh really got a big heart, yuh know dat?

She sucks her teeth. Leaves shop.

Scene 17

Int. Fish and chip shop. Day.

MISS MAY *inspecting the till.*

MISS MAY: Is dis all de money you collected, boy? Is dis all de money, Desmon'? What's wrong wit' you youn' people? Yuh'd steal from yuh own modder?

DESMOND (*defiantly*): I an' I din steal not a damn t'ing.

MISS MAY: Doan use dat kind uh language to me, boy. (*Pause*) Yuh hear me? (*Pause.* DESMOND *defiant*) What am I gun do wit' you, boy? (*Pause*)

Scene 18

Int. No. 35 Empire Road. Night.

We see the KAPOORS' *front room. It is being used as a sort of mini temple. We see* MR KAPOOR *kneeling, praying. The door behind him opens silently.* RANJANAA *pokes her head in. Observes her father. Disappears. Shuts door quietly.*

Scene 19

Int. KAPOORS' *hallway.*

We see RANJANAA *lean against one wall of hallway. She closes her eyes, a trapped bird.*

Scene 20

Int. EVERTON'S *living-room. Night.*

EVERTON *and* MARCUS *watching TV.*

EVERTON: O rant. I own a whole shop dat you could have tomorrow if dat's what yuh want. But not you.

MARCUS (*joshingly*): Dad ... yuh listenin' to me or not, eh? Ah tole you a hundred times. I got to do things my way.

EVERTON: You doan appreciate my help.

MARCUS (*as before*): What? Course I appreciate your help.

EVERTON: What sort uh job is dat for a good West Indian boy? Dry cleaner!

MARCUS: Yuh radder ah was a boxer? Or a singer in a calypso band?

EVERTON: Tell me again.

MARCUS: Ah've already told you.

> HORTENSE *enters.*

HORTENSE: What you two fightin' about?

MARCUS: We not fightin'. We both want de same thing, dat's all. We both want to run my life.

EVERTON: Ah doan want to run your life.

MARCUS (*amused*): Course you do, Dad.

EVERTON (*to* HORTENSE): Has 'e tole you yet? He's back to 'is ole job. Dat dirty, smelly dry cleanin' shop in Grove Street.

HORTENSE: Dat place. Lord.

EVERTON: Rapid, dey call it. Rapid Dry Cleaners. Takes dem two weeks to dry clean one pair uh socks. Imagine how long it takes dem to do a suit.

MARCUS: Thank you, Bob Hope. (*To* HORTENSE) Ah want to learn de dry cleanin' business. You know ah want to buy dat old shop. If it's good enough fo' Jewish people, it's good enough fo' me.

EVERTON: What sort uh son is dis? Dis boy loves everybody. Jews, Asians, Communists, everybody. Mark my words. One day he'll bring home a Pakistani an' 'e'll tell us, 'Meet my wife'.

HORTENSE: Ev-er-ton. Doan say dat. Not even as a joke. Son, yuh fadder doan really mean dat.

MARCUS (*leaving room*): Ah give up.

Scene 21
Int. Rapid Dry Cleaning Shop. Day.

> *Small and unprepossessing to say the least. We see* MARCUS *dealing with a* CUSTOMER. CUSTOMER *leaves.* MARCUS *continues writing out dry cleaning list. Someone enters shop. He looks up. We see his face. Then we see who it is.* RANJANAA. *Plus one dress in a bag for cleaning.*

MARCUS: Hello! What brings you here?

> *She presents dress to him.*

RANJANAA: You do dry cleaning, don't you?

> *Pause.*

MARCUS: Jus' one dress?

RANJANAA: Can't they clean just one dress?

MARCUS: Matches your eyes, doesn't it? Are yuh going to wear it at the party on Saturday?

RANJANAA: When can I pick it up?

He hands her ticket.

MARCUS: Be ready on Friday. Late afternoon. Tell me ... How come you come all this way passin' all dose other dry cleaners, jus' to bring me one dress?

RANJANAA (*at door*):   I've tried the best, I thought I'd give the worst a chance.

He laughs, but she has already left.

Scene 22

Int. EVERTON'S *living-room. Night.*

EVERTON *reading encyclopaedia.* WALTER *reading* Reveille.

WALTER: Eh, eh. (*He tut-tuts.*) D-disgustin'. (*Head in paper*) Ah doan understan' dis sortuh thing at all.

EVERTON: Walter, ah'm tryin' to read.

WALTER: Sez here. A woman te-teachuh wants to marry a t-twelve-year-old boy. His *mistress* who is eleven is ob-objectin'! De teachuh is f-fifty. What sortuh s-school is dat?

Pause. EVERTON *just looks at him.*

EVERTON: Walter, Willum Shakespeare said some people are born mad, an' some have madness t'rust upon dem. What's your excuse? (*The doorbell rings.*) Now what? Yuh reckon it's de dog catchers comin' fo' you? Hortense!

There is no reply. EVERTON *gets up grudgingly and leaves living-room.*

Scene 23

Int. Hall and front door. Night.

EVERTON *goes to answer the door. He opens the door to* DESMOND *and* ROYSTON REID.

EVERTON: Oh God.

DESMOND: Greetin's.

EVERTON: Greetings?! It's not Chrismus yet.

DESMOND: I an' I would like to come in.

EVERTON: What for? (*Then*) I an' I?!

DESMOND: M'modder send dis, de rent.

He holds up dirty rentbook.

EVERTON: Rent? That's good. She's a day early. Enter. (*He lets them into hall. They make as if to enter the living-room.*) Hold yuh horse, sonny. (*Great smile*) No offence, but my livin'-room is fo' frien's. We can do our business right here.

DESMOND: Okay, suh. Dis month's rent.

EVERTON (*about* ROYSTON):   Doan he talk?

DESMOND: Say hello, Royston.

ROYSTON (*like he's looking for a fight*): Hello.

> EVERTON *steps back, gives him a look.*

DESMOND: Suh, I an' I got a favour to ax you. We want a job, suh.

EVERTON: You want what?

DESMOND: Work.

EVERTON: Say dat word again.

DESMOND: Work.

EVERTON: Ah doan believe it.

DESMOND: Them English people doan want to give us no work.

EVERTON: Dat surprises yuh, does it?

DESMOND: Help us get a job, mahn.

EVERTON: Me? Me?

DESMOND: Youse de Godfadder, suh.

EVERTON: De who?

DESMOND: Das what dey calls you in Han'swort'.[11] Godfadder.

EVERTON: De Godfadder. Who – me?

DESMOND: Help us, mahn.

EVERTON: De Godfadder. Yeah? (*Then*) Anyway, you don't want to work.

DESMOND: Yes, mahn. Any job dat pays a lot uh money.

EVERTON: A job dat pays a lot uh money, eh? Yuh want a good lash, dat's what yuh want.

DESMOND: I an' I want to be like you. A rich mahn.

EVERTON: Leave my house. Go on.

> *He opens the front door. A beat.*

DESMOND: Help us, suh. Any job. You could help if yuh want.

> *A beat.* DESMOND *and* ROYSTON *go.* EVERTON *closes door after them. He does not move. Pause.*

HORTENSE (*off*):   Everton?

> HORTENSE *appears.*

HORTENSE: Who was dat?

EVERTON (*almost to himself*):   De Godfadder, eh? Nice, nice.

---

[11] *Han'swort'*: Handsworth, a multi-racial area of Birmingham.

Scene 24

Int. Rapid Dry Cleaners. Day.

RANJANAA *enters. Is in a hurry, what with it being Friday and all.*

RANJANAA: Come to collect my dress.

MARCUS (*producing dress*):   An' to see me, ah hope.

RANJANAA: How much is it, please?

MARCUS: What's the matter?

RANJANAA: I've got shopping to do before the shops shut.

MARCUS: Can't you spare five minutes?

RANJANAA: I didn't know your father was our landlord.

MARCUS: Aren't you lucky? (*She smiles at him.*) How long have you lived in Englan'?

RANJANAA: Since I was nine. And you?

MARCUS: Forever.

Another CUSTOMER *enters, inhibiting* MARCUS *and* RANJANAA.

RANJANAA: Yes, well. Must go. How much is it?

MARCUS: Fifty pence. (*She pays him.*) Ah'll see you tomorrow, won't I ... at the street party?

RANJANAA: I'll be around. 'Bye.

She goes.

Scene 25

Int. EVERTON's *shop. Day.*

EVERTON *and* WALTER *in the shop, plus four or five* CUSTOMERS – *West Indian and Asian.* EVERTON *dealing with* TWO FAT WEST INDIAN WOMEN.

EVERTON: Mauby bark?[12] Yes, sure. Walter. Mauby bark.

WALTER *locates a packet of mauby bark and brings it over.*

EVERTON: Thanks. (*To* CUSTOMERS) Anything else, ladies?

One of them shakes her head, no. She pays EVERTON. DESMOND *and* ROYSTON *enter the shop. They drift in as if bent on crime.* EVERTON *is immediately on guard.*

EVERTON: Can ah do anything fo' you gentlemen?

DESMOND *wanders over.* WALTER *keeps an eye on* ROYSTON.

DESMOND: What's up?

EVERTON: What's up where?

---

[12] *Mauby bark*: bark from which a bitter-sweet drink is made.

DESMOND *sees* WALTER *is keeping an eye on* ROYSTON.

DESMOND: He's not g'un steal nothin'.

EVERTON: Doan tell me dat, tell *him* dat.

DESMOND (*not looking away from* EVERTON): Royston. (ROYSTON *approaches*.) Wait fo' me outside.

ROYSTON *sucks his teeth but goes all the same. A beat.*

EVERTON: How many 'A' levels has he got? (*He chuckles to himself, pleased as punch with his own wit.*)

DESMOND: I come again. (EVERTON *looks as if he wants to laugh*.) You laugh at I an' my brodder but it's not funny.

A beat. EVERTON *serious.*

DESMOND: Again I ax fo' yuh help. M'modder she work too hard, boss. Gimme a job here.

EVERTON: Here? You?

DESMOND: Why not, mahn? I is a strong mahn.

Scene 26
Int. RANJANAA's *room. Night.*

RANJANAA *sitting at a sewing machine, sewing – sewing decorations for the street party.* MR KAPOOR *enters.*

MR KAPOOR: Ranjanaa, what you doin'?

RANJANAA: Sewing.

MR KAPOOR: I'm not blind.

RANJANAA: I'm sewing decorations for the street party tomorrow.

MR KAPOOR: Is that our business? *Their* party, in street?

Scene 27
Int. EVERTON's *shop. Day.*

EVERTON *is calling someone (off) in the back room of the shop. A* CUSTOMER *about.*

EVERTON: Come on, come on. Where're you, Dr Who?

DESMOND *appears from the back room.* EVERTON *has him wearing a large apron, like a butcher's apron.* DESMOND *is carrying a number of tins of a product known as 'Nutriment'.* EVERTON *takes two from him.*

EVERTON: Always make sure we got lots uh dis in stock. Older West Indians love 'Nutriment'. Gives dem energy. (*To* CUSTOMER) Madam.

WOMAN *takes two tins of 'Nutriment' from him.* EVERTON *goes to till,* WOMAN *pays, he rings up sale. We see* DESMOND *looking at the contents of till, at the money.* EVERTON *looks at him.* DESMOND *looks guiltily away.* CUSTOMER *leaves.*

EVERTON: Doan forget, Desmon'. You're on trial. Work hard an' you're okay. One slip-up an' yuh back on the street. (*Pause*) Now, what's dis about you wantin' to leave early dis afternoon? Your first day at work an' you want to go early? Anyway, ah dunno what yuh want to go dere for. I wouldn't be seen *dead* at a street party.

Scene 28
Ext. Street party. Day.

    EVERTON *at street party, obviously having a good time...*

Scene 29
Ext. Parking lot. Street party. Afternoon.

    Late afternoon. Nearly everybody from Empire Road is there. A steel band.

Scene 30
Ext. Street party. Afternoon.

    We see party from another vantage point. We see MARCUS *helping out at ice-cream section. Helping* KATE MORRIS. *He is sharing out choc-ices to a number of children, West Indian, Asian, English, all working class. Kids jumping up and down.*

KATE: Oh God! We're going to run out of these damn things. I better go and get some more.

MARCUS: Ah rather you found me some bouncers to protect me from this lot.

    KATE *sees* RANJANAA.

KATE: Ranju! Come and give Marcus a hand.

    RANJANAA *comes over.*

KATE: I've got to get some more ice-cream.

    KATE *goes.*

RANJANAA: I was looking for you.
1ST KID: You gave him two!
MARCUS (*to* RANJANAA): What?
RANJANAA: I said—
2ND KID (*to* 1ST KID): No, I never.

1ST KID: Yes, you have.
MARCUS: Order! Let's have some order around here!

Scene 31
Ext. Party. Afternoon.

> *We see* EVERTON *surrounded by a number of middle-aged working-class* WOMEN, *many white.*

EVERTON: . . . so the man buys a guide to good restaurants. Inside dere's dis restaurant which claims dat dey would serve any dish requested. So he visits dis restaurant. He orders rhinoceros toes on toast.
ONE OF THE WOMEN: Rhinoceros toes on toast!
EVERTON: *Fried* rhinoceros toes on toast. Anyway de waiter doesn't bat an eyelid. He disappears into kitchen wit' de order. But in a minute he's back again. 'I'm sorry, sir,' says de waiter, 'we're fresh out of bread!'

Scene 32
Ext. Party. Afternoon.

> *Reggae music. People dancing.* DESMOND *enjoying himself, surrounded by* ROYSTON *and admiring* FRIENDS.

DESMOND (*about guitar player*):   Him is strictly roots![13]

Scene 33
Ext. Street party. Later.

> *A conga line has started.* EVERTON *leading,* HORTENSE *behind him. As conga line swerves,* EVERTON *sees* RANJANAA *and* MARCUS *together.* MARCUS *is trying to pull* RANJANAA *into conga line.* EVERTON *struck by something going on between them. Turns to* HORTENSE.

EVERTON: Look at your son. Wit' Miss Sari. Ah told you. Dat boy is a liberal.

> MARCUS *and* RANJANAA *have now joined conga line. Suddenly we see* MR KAPOOR *from another angle. He is walking towards party when, horrified, he sees* MARCUS's *arms around his daughter. He strides forward, grabs his daughter and pulls her away.* MARCUS *too stunned to move. The conga continues.*
>
> *We pull back to see party. We see* KAPOOR *and* RANJANAA *walking away. Bring up theme song over this. Conga moves away leaving* MARCUS *standing alone.*

---

[13] *strictly roots*: real, basic reggae.

SUGGESTIONS FOR WRITING AND DISCUSSION

1 *Outline the main strands of plot suggested in this opening episode of* Empire Road. *How successful do you think these are in arousing interest in viewers so that they will want to see another episode?*

2 *Give accounts of the impressions you get of the main characters. Say why you might be interested in finding out how they cope with another situation.*

3 *Try to analyse what is comic in this play, taking into account character, situation and verbal play.*

4 *Describe the racial attitudes revealed by different characters and comment on them (for example, Hortense and Everton's attitudes to Indians, and Marcus's attitude to people of other races).*

5 *What are your views on racial jokes and on race as a basis for comedy?*

6 *Comment on the way this episode ends. Do you think it is an effective way to end a first episode and would it make you want to watch further episodes?*

7 *Why do you think this play might appeal particularly to black viewers/readers? What would you say there is about it that all viewers/readers might enjoy?*

8 *Choose two scenes that you think work particularly well in televisual terms and explain why.*

9 *Using this play as an example, describe some of the things a television play can do that a novel or a stage play cannot. Would you say these are advantages or not?*

10 *Compare this play with an episode from another situation comedy you have seen recently on television.*

11 *Write a story or a play in which someone's parents disapprove of his or her friends.*

12 *Write a story or a play in which someone tries to get a job.*

13 *Do you think enough time is given on television to black programmes? Imagine that you are a producer for one of the television channels. What further black programmes would you plan? Give the outline of the planned programme(s) as fully as you can.*

14 *Write about any programme you have watched which has black presenters or actors (for example,* Black on Black, Ebony, No Problem*). Outline what the programme is about and say how successful you think it is.*

15 *Compare the way two of the characters speak (for instance, Desmond and Marcus). What do you think a television play like this gains from having characters who speak different dialects of English?*

16 *Improvise a situation where a son or daughter announces that he or she wants to marry someone the family utterly disapproves of.*

17 *When you have acted out the above improvisation, write a script for it.*

18 *Discuss how Abbensetts uses the themes of generation difference and race in this episode.*

EMPIRE ROAD

ROYSTON'S DAY

CHARACTERS

EVERTON
HORTENSE
MARCUS
WALTER
DESMOND
ROYSTON
MISS MAY
RANJANAA
KATE MORRIS
SHELLEY
FOSTER
RENTON

EXTRAS

Two white club bouncers
White couple at club
Ticket girl at club
Two white girls at club
White policeman
Shop customers

This is Episode 4 of *Empire Road*. Walter has now married Miss May, and Ranjanaa has moved into a bed-sit away from her father.

Scene 1

Int. Club. Hallway. Night.

The entrance hall of a small club in Birmingham. The club itself is down the stairs. We can hear music. There is a GIRL *in a cubicle selling tickets. But before you can get to her a* YOUNG WHITE COUPLE *arrive. Neither is specially dressed but they are not scruffy either. The* YOUNG MAN *is wearing a jacket and jeans.*

Then DESMOND *and* ROYSTON *arrive. We see them from* FOSTER's *point of view. They wear wool caps, jumble-sale windbreaker-type jackets.* FOSTER *immediately bars their way.*

FOSTER: Sorry, members only.

DESMOND: What? Dis dirty ole club. On your bike.

FOSTER: If yer not a member, yer not welcome.

DESMOND: Do yuh stop everybody or jus' us?

FOSTER: My job is to prevent trouble. An' that's what you two look like to me. Trouble.

DESMOND: I is not a member but m'brodder here is a member.

FOSTER: Prove it.

DESMOND: Show dis man yuh membership card, Royston. Man here is an infidel. An unbeliever. (ROYSTON *searches his pockets slowly.*) He likes to take his time. He's very thorough. Dat's what dey say on him report card. Royston is thorough. Thoroughly stupid.

DESMOND snickers, laughs, ROYSTON as well.

FOSTER: Look, why don't you boys go back to your neighbourhood? Where you two from? Sunny Thornley? (*He laughs a little.*) The Sunshine State. (*To* GIRL *selling tickets*) Hey, Viv, you 'eard this one? One of our young Commonwealth brethren – you know the sort, tea-cosies on their heads, braids down to the ankles. Anyway our jungle bunnie was walking down the street with a pig over 'is shoulder. A copper spots 'im, stops 'im and says, 'Where d'youw find that?' So the pig replies, 'I bouwght 'im in a raffle.'

DESMOND (*to* ROYSTON): Man here's a joker. Laugh. Make him happy.

ROYSTON obliges with threatening laugh. Then attacks FOSTER.

ROYSTON: Jah! Jah! Jah!

DESMOND: Let's go.

DESMOND starts to run. FOSTER *grabs* ROYSTON, *holds on.* ROYSTON *can't shake him off.*

FOSTER: At least I got one of youse.

Scene 2

Int. MISS MAY's *house. Night.*

MISS MAY *and* WALTER *in bed. They have only been married a few weeks.* MISS MAY *is fast asleep.* WALTER *is awake. He is awake because he is cold. He is cold because* MISS MAY *has hogged all the blankets. We see* WALTER *trying to get some of the covers away from her. He is trying to do so without waking her. He tries to pull a bit of the blanket. No go. He tries again. No go. Suddenly she wakes up.*

MISS MAY (*irritably*):   Walter, boy, why yuh playin' games in de middle of de night?

WALTER: Yuh got all de b-b-blankets.

MISS MAY (*sucking her teeth*):   Dat's why you wake me up? Jus' cos of a little bit uh blanket?

WALTER: Ah'm cold.

MISS MAY: Walter, I wouldn't t'ink of *wakin'* you up in de middle of de night, not even if I was cold as a ice-berg.

WALTER: Yes, b-but you're de one wit' all de b-blanket.

MISS MAY: Look, Walter, if you gonna start a row now in de middle of de night jus' tell me, an' ah'll go an' sleep in de kitchen.

Pause. Suddenly there is a knocking on the bedroom door.

MISS MAY: Who's dat?

DESMOND (*off*):   It is I, Desmon'.

MISS MAY: Yuh crazy or what, boy?

DESMOND (*off*):   It's Royston. 'E get arrested.

MISS MAY (*sitting up*):   Arrested? Royston?

WALTER (*heavenwards*):   Oh God.

Scene 3

Int. EVERTON's *shop. Morning.*

EVERTON *alone in the shop. A* CUSTOMER *comes in. Selects a carton of orange juice. Pays. Goes.* DESMOND *arrives.*

EVERTON: Boy, what time yuh call dis?

DESMOND: M'brodder get arrested.

A beat.

EVERTON: Is dat good or bad?

Scene 4

Int. MISS MAY's *kitchen. Day.*

WALTER *is trying to leave.*

MISS MAY: Come wit' me.

WALTER: You're his m-modder, not me. Ah gone.

MISS MAY: Ah doan trus' de police. Look at de way I had to ring dem. Dey didn't even ring me.

WALTER: It's only de g-guilty who need fear de police. Not de innoc-cent.

MISS MAY: Oh, yes? Yuh jus' like a chile, Walter. I afraid uh dem. If yuh black, dey got a way of lookin' at yuh. Terrible, terrible. Come wit' me to de police station, Walter. I afraid uh dem.

WALTER: I'll w-walk wit' you as far as de s-s-station. But ah can't go in.

Scene 5

Int. EVERTON's *back room. Day.*

EVERTON: An' where is Walter? Doan tell me he's bin arrested as well?

DESMOND: Walter? Dat'll be de day. (*Then*) Godfadder...

EVERTON: Ah doan wish to know.

Pause.

DESMOND: Him not very smart, ah know dat. Him ain' learnin' not'in' in school. Yuh know what Royston get to look forward to? Eh? A life in a fact'ry. It's eidder dat or no work at all. Help 'im, suh. Please, Godfadder.

EVERTON: Yuh brodder is prison material. I got better things to do wit' my time dan help a boy who got no more future dan a long prison sentence.

Scene 6

Ext. Thornley police station. Day.

We see WALTER *and* MISS MAY *approach the police station. They stop outside.* MISS MAY *says something to him.* WALTER *shakes his head, no. She goes in alone.*

Scene 7

Int. EVERTON's *shop. Day.*

EVERTON *is writing something down.*

DESMOND: Godfadder.

EVERTON (*not looking up*):   Ah said no.

DESMOND: Dey gun come fo' me as well. Sooner or later. De police. (EVERTON *looks up.*) Yuh gun jus' stan' by an' let dem arrest me as well?

EVERTON: Why not? What yuh expec' me to do? Slip into m'Batman costume an' beat hell outa dem when dey come fo' you?

Pause. WALTER *arrives.*

EVERTON: Oh, rant. Oh, rant. Mr Early Bird. Ah'm surprised yuh boddered to turn up at all. Don't think ah don't appreciate it, cos ah don't.

Scene 8
Ext. School playground. Day.

> A *number of* TEENAGERS *surrounding* MISS MORRIS. *The* TEENAGERS *improvise talk to* MISS MORRIS.
>
> *Then she sees a fight starting up between two 12/13-year-olds. She breaks it up and sends children back to classes. As she follows them in* MISS MAY *appears.*

MISS MAY: Miss! Miss! Dey got m'son.
KATE: What's this?
MISS MAY: Dey pick on we! Pick on we. No love. No love. All uh you – yuh with yer nice, soft job an' yuh doan help, yuh doan help. Not even you! No help at all.
KATE: What's happened, luv?
MISS MAY: Dey got m'son, jus' like m'first husband. Yuh doan do any damn good, none uh yuh. All the same. Police, lawyers, teachers.
KATE: All right, all right. Which son? Who is your son, luv?
MISS MAY: Royston, dey arrested Royston.
KATE: Oh, you're Mrs Reid.
MISS MAY: I's Mrs Isaacs now.
KATE: Well, Mrs Isaacs. What has Royston been up to now?

Scene 9
Int. School staircase. Day.

KATE: Mrs Isaacs, the police have a right to hold Royston for twenty-four hours before bringing charges. – Haven't you kids got a class to go to? – From what you say they are probably going to charge him with assault.
MISS MAY: Yeh, dey told me dat at de station. But my son is a good boy. He wouldn't assault nobody. (CHILDREN *enter.*)
KATE: Haven't you two got a class to go to? – Mrs Isaacs, there was a witness.
MISS MAY: What should I do about a lawyer, Miss?
KATE: You are entitled to legal aid.
MISS MAY: Legal aid. Dat's for hippies.
KATE *(laughing)*:   Hippies! Hippies! Oh, Mrs Isaacs.
MISS MAY: No legal aid fo' me. I want a proper lawyer.
KATE: *And* who is going to pay for this 'proper' lawyer?
MISS MAY *(pause)*:   At de police station 'e kept sayin' ah love yuh, Modder. Modder, ah sorry. Modder, ah love yuh. (*Pause*) Dey fadder left me when Desmon' was four an' Royston was only three. Royston always had it worse

of all. (*A beat*) Ah gotta get 'im a good law-yuh.

KATE (*gently*):   It's going to cost a lot of money. Where will you find the money?

MISS MAY: Chile, I's so tired of being poor. Lord. (*Then*) Ah'll have to borrow it from somewhere.

Scene 10

Int. EVERTON's *house. Kitchenette. Night.*

> *At first we just see* EVERTON *at dinner. He has a pork chop and peas 'n' rice in front of him. But he is not eating. He is at present cutting up an apple. He then puts a piece of pork, some rice and a slice of apple in his mouth, eats. Camera pulls away and we see* HORTENSE *at other end of the table. She is also eating pork, rice 'n' peas. But no apple.*

HORTENSE: Boy, after all dese years ah still find you strange. Ah mean sure ah know some people like to eat apple wit' dey salad. But wit' dey *rice 'n' peas* – never.

> EVERTON *spears another piece of apple on his fork, holds it near his mouth.*

EVERTON: Apples give me rosy cheeks.

> *He pops apple in his mouth. Phone rings.* HORTENSE *gets up and answers it.*

HORTENSE: T'ree – oh – double five – oh, Walter . . . now? . . . well . . . well, ah dunno, ah mean, look, hole on, hole on . . . It's Walter. He wants to know if 'e can come over an' bring her wit' 'im. (*She makes a face.*)

EVERTON (*a bit naughty here*):   Her. Who?

HORTENSE: Ev-er-ton. Yuh know who. His wife.

EVERTON: Oh, rant. Ah can hardly wait.

HORTENSE: Hello, Walter, it's awright, bring 'er ovah, but not fo' long, yuh hear me, maybe five, six minutes. (EVERTON *laughs as she hangs up. She isn't amused.*) Ah know it's only de firse time . . . but ah hope she doan make a habit of it.

Scene 11

Int. Ranjanaa's bedsit. Night.

MARCUS: Looks an' smells fantastic.

RANJANAA: I don't know why. It's nothing special.

MARCUS: Course it is. It's for me, isn't it? It must be special.

RANJANAA: Big head.

MARCUS: Tell me again what it is.

Scene 12

Int. EVERTON's *living-room. Night.*

EVERTON, HORTENSE, WALTER *and* MISS MAY. HORTENSE *still standing.*

EVERTON: Wonderloaf! Wonderloaf!

MISS MAY (*to* WALTER):   He's always dis crazy?

EVERTON: To say we're happy to see you is de understatement of de year. Where's dat dress of yours, Wonderloaf?

MISS MAY: What dress?

EVERTON: De dress yuh wore at yuh weddin' reception. Dat wonderful creation.

HORTENSE (*interrupting*):   Will yuh have a little sherry? Some white wine, chilled white wine or rum, brandy? Take yuh pick. I don't drink, of course.

A beat.

EVERTON: Give 'er a little of everything, dear, Scotch, gin, white wine, sherry, Coke-a-Cola, de lot. In a mug. Wit' a straw. (*To* MISS MAY) Would yuh like dat, Big Ben?

HORTENSE (*to* MISS MAY):   He's a han'ful, isn't 'e?

She smiles fondly at EVERTON.

Scene 13

Int. RANJANAA's *bedsit. Night.*

RANJANAA *has got something in her hair. She is bending over. Her hair falling forwards. She removes whatever it is that's in her hair, then throws her head back, gives her long hair a shake.*

MARCUS: That was delicious.

RANJANAA: My pleasure.

He is looking at her. She is disconcerted and starts to leave the room.

MARCUS: Where're you goin'?

RANJANAA: To wash up.

MARCUS: Do it later. Jus' sit down. (*She sits down again, but as far away from him as possible.*) Can't you sit any further away than that? Takin' it a bit far, aren't you? Keep on being so proper an' we could get you a job in the Vatican.

RANJANAA: It's all very well for you, Marcus. Indian girls aren't like English girls.

MARCUS: I'm not an English girl.

RANJANAA: It's not funny.

MARCUS: Sorry, I know you're not like other girls. That's why you're special.

RANJANAA: Tell me you love me.

MARCUS: You know I do.

RANJANAA: Well, say it. Tell me.

MARCUS: I love you so much.

They rise. He leads her to bedroom. Door closes after them.

Scene 14

Int. EVERTON's *living-room. Night.*

Everybody has a drink now. HORTENSE *is seated, a Coke beside her.*

HORTENSE: So ... May ... m'brodder was tellin' me yuh was married before. How many times?

MISS MAY: Only once.

HORTENSE: Well, ah'm glad yuh doan make a habit of it.

MISS MAY: Habit? I doan make a habit of gettin' married.

HORTENSE (*so innocently surprised*): She's takin' offence. Walter, yuh wife is takin' offence. Tell 'er ah doan mean no harm, ah jus believe in plain speakin'.

WALTER (*to* MAY): Dear, ah doan t-think—

MISS MAY: Ah know yuh doan think, yuh can't.

EVERTON (*smiling happily*): Oh, score! Dey havin' dey firse tiff.

WALTER *and* MISS MAY *are looking at each other.*

HORTENSE: It's all my fault. Ah din mean no harm. I apologize, May.

MISS MAY *sucks her teeth under her breath, then turns away.*

EVERTON: So, Walter, how's married life? You show me your scars an' ah'll show you mine.

HORTENSE: Ev-er-ton.

EVERTON (*rubbing his hands together, very pleased with his patter*): Oh, score! Oh, score!

HORTENSE (*so friendly*): May, ah want to ask you something about dat fish 'n' chip shop you run dere. How late you stay open at night?

MISS MAY: Sometimes till eleven, twelve o'clock.

HORTENSE: Midnight? (*Turning to* EVERTON) Yuh hear dat, Everton?

MISS MAY: Ah doan *like* workin' late. Haven't you never had to work at a night job?

HORTENSE: Me! Out on an English street late at night? Oh, Chrismus. I would *die.* All dem flashers an' rapers.

MISS MAY: Ah got two sons, ah got to take whatever job ah get.

HORTENSE: An' ah respec' yuh for it, May. Ask Everton. Everton, doan I respec' May? (*Pause. Back to* MISS MAY.) But a West Indian fish 'n' chip lady ...! Dat could get you into de *Guinness Book of Records.*

MISS MAY: De *Guinness Book of Records?* What's dat, Walter?

It is time for them to talk about the reason for her being there. WALTER *clears his throat.*

WALTER: Am, Everton. (*He clears his throat again.*) Am. M-May here has s-s-something she w-wants to ask you.

EVERTON: Oh, yes?

MISS MAY: About m'son.

EVERTON: Oh, yes?

MISS MAY (*suddenly breaking*):   Oh God, ah'm in trouble, bad trouble, ah got no money, ah can't feed dem *and* pay fo' a lawyuh for dem as well. Ah not askin' fo' no free gift, ah'll pay yuh back, every penny, but help me, Mr Bennett, help me, man.

> *Close-up of* EVERTON: *a man backed into a corner. Pause.*

Scene 15

Ext. Broad Street, Birmingham. Day.

> *Lunchtime.* RANJANAA *leaves the office where she works. Walks down street.* SHELLEY, *one of the other girls from same office, catches up with her.* SHELLEY: *English, Brummy accent.*

SHELLEY: Hold up. Us girls are goin' to the pub after work this evenin'. You know Trish, don't you?

RANJANAA: Trish?

SHELLEY: Course you do. Anyway, it's 'er birthday.

RANJANAA: I'm sorry. I do not go into pubs. I'm sorry.

SHELLEY: Don't go into pubs? What else is there to do? You know your trouble, don't you? You work too hard. I know you're new in the office but some of the girls have remarked on the fact that you're – well, too *eager*. (*A beat*) Know what I mean, our kid? (*Pause*) You like Diana Ross?

Scene 16

Int. Police station. Back room. Day.

> EVERTON *and* ROYSTON. ROYSTON *looking tough, sullen, unkempt. At first he just remains silent, which doesn't please* EVERTON. *Pause. Finally.*

EVERTON: Yuh're not a load uh laughs, are you?

ROYSTON: Dey doan like me an' I doan like dem.

EVERTON: Pardon?

ROYSTON: Dey afraid of I.

EVERTON: Dey afraid of you, are dey?

ROYSTON: Godfadder.

EVERTON: What?

ROYSTON: Dat's what him calls you. Desmon'. Godfadder.

> *A beat.*

EVERTON: Tell me something. Why do you two talk like Jamaicans. Rastafari? Have you even seen Jamaica?

ROYSTON: No, sur.

EVERTON: You were born here, weren't you? Right here in Birmin'ham.

ROYSTON: Right, our kid.

EVERTON: Oh, rant. Oh, rant. Yet you prefer to soun' like yuh jus' come from Jamaica. Why, boy, why?

ROYSTON: Cos dey hate I. Him in dat uniform out dere, dey hate we. I jus' sixteen years ole, yet dey hate I.

EVERTON: Boy, why yuh doan pull yuhself togedder? Instead of always complainin' how badly dey hate you. Smarten up.

ROYSTON: You doan like I, eidder. Do you? Right? Right?

EVERTON: Maybe ah'm gettin' too old, but jus' lookin' at you, yuh upset me, boy. To any sort uh decent, hard-workin' West Indian, a boy like you is a slap in de face. Look at yuh. Why should I help you?

ROYSTON (*on his feet*): Cha, man. You mek I sick. Get away.

EVERTON: You're no damn Rastafarian. I an' I, all dat junk. Talk normal like everybody else.

ROYSTON: Stupid ole man!

EVERTON: Ah wouldn't help you across de street!

Scene 17

Int. MISS MAY's *fish 'n' chip shop. Day.*

MISS MAY *is taking off her coat in the back room.*

MISS MAY: Ah not open fo' business yet. (*We see that* EVERTON *has entered.*)

EVERTON (*quietly*): It's me, May.

MISS MAY (*full of sudden hope*): Yuh see 'im. Dey let you see 'im?

EVERTON: Yes, ah saw 'im.

MISS MAY: *And?*

EVERTON: Look, ah've changed m'mind. Ah can't help dat boy.

MISS MAY: Doan say dat.

EVERTON: Yes, well, ah'm sorry.

MISS MAY: Ah got nobody else to turn to.

EVERTON: My mind's made up.

MISS MAY: But why? Did 'e insult you? Ah'll beat 'im if 'e insult yuh.

EVERTON: He din insult me, May. He's jus' a fool to 'imself.

MISS MAY: Dat's why he needs yuh help more. 'E's not very bright but 'e's got a big heart.

EVERTON: A big heart? Who we talkin' about, Royston or Lassie de Wonder Dog?

A beat.

MISS MAY: Youse a real, nasty piece uh work, yuh know dat, Mr Bennett.

EVERTON: Ah've never said ah was perfec', Miss May.

MISS MAY: You're all jus' prejudice against m'son, he doan have a chance!

EVERTON: He's 'is own worse enemy. What'll happen to 'im when 'e leaves school, eh? It's a boxin' ring out dere. Look at Soho Road. An' lots of odder streets in Birmin'ham. All dose young black men livin' all day in de bettin' shops. No work, no prospects, a big zero. A bloody boxin' ring. But de only way yuh gonna survive in any boxin' ring is to fight back. Fight, fight, fight. Ah know dey want to sen' us back where we come from. Ah'm not stupid. But dere must be more *constructive* ways to fight back dan t'rowin' stones at de police or attackin' ole ladies.

MISS MAY: My son don't attack ole ladies. What you sayin'? Take dat back. Yuh got no right to wish such a future on him!

EVERTON: Ah wouldn't wish such a future on any man. But show me 'is frien's an' ah'll show you 'is future.

Pause.

MISS MAY (*quiet pain*):   He's my son. My son. What yuh want me to do? Put 'im out de house? Kick 'im out on de street wit' all dose odder bettin' shop bums? Ah can't jus' cut 'im out of m'heart. He's m'flesh an' blood.

Pause. EVERTON *exits.*

MISS MAY: Oh Lord. Oh Lord.

Scene 18

Int. MISS MAY's *kitchen. Night.*

DESMOND *singing and playing his guitar:* 'I Shot the Sheriff'. *He sings for a few moments. Then the door opens and* MISS MAY *enters. He stops playing.*

MISS MAY: Desmon', oh God, dey here. Dey come fo' you.

DESMOND: Who?

A POLICEMAN *appears behind his mother's back. Close-up of* DESMOND.

Scene 19

Int. EVERTON's *living-room. Midday.*

HORTENSE *filling two bowls with nuts.* MARCUS *and* RANJANAA *expected any moment.* EVERTON *enters, wearing a tie.*

EVERTON: Pass me some uh dem nuts, please. When's yuh son bringin' dat girl, ah'm starvin'. (*He suddenly laughs.*)

HORTENSE: Boy, what you laughin' at, eh?

EVERTON: Ah remember one day goin' to see Sam Chase. You know dat comedian. Was in Georgetown.[1] Jus' before he died. Ah remember 'e asked a woman dis question. Oh, score! What's de capital of Hungary?

---

[1] *Georgetown*: the capital of Guyana.

HORTENSE: De capital of where?

EVERTON: Hungary. An' de woman din know, an' 'e tell 'er 'starvation'. (*He drums his feet on the floor.*) Oh, score! Oh, score!

HORTENSE: Everton, yuh too foolish really.

EVERTON: De capital of Hungary. Starvation.

HORTENSE: Ah wish I could laugh. We got dis girl comin' as well. Ah not lookin' forward to dis meal.

EVERTON: De girl's okay. She can't help it if she's Indian.

HORTENSE: Ah still doan understan' dis. An Indian girl, it doan seem right. (*Doorbell rings.*) Ah! Here they are.

Scene 20

Int. MISS MAY's *kitchen. Day.*

> *We see* WALTER *at sink washing up some cups and saucers. Still in dressing-gown. Looks very unloved.*
> *Sound of front door.* MISS MAY *enters. Has been to church. She's a Baptist. She is preoccupied with her own troubles.*

WALTER: How was ch-ch-church?

MISS MAY: M'boys. Ah prayed fo' dem. Fo' bot' m'sons.

WALTER: You look t-t-tired. Why-why-why don't you sit down?

MISS MAY: Yes. (*She sits.*)

WALTER: Tell yuh w-what. Ah'll cook de Sun-Sun-Sunday dinner.

MISS MAY: Yuh mean it?

Scene 21

Int. EVERTON's *living-room. Day.*

> RANJANAA *and* MARCUS *have arrived.*

MARCUS (*to* EVERTON, *laughing*):   No, we came by taxi. She's still frightened her father'll see her.

HORTENSE: Marcus, ah'm waitin' for you to introduce me.

MARCUS: Sorry. Mother, I'd like you to meet Ranjanaa Kapoor.

RANJANAA: I'm very pleased to meet you, Mrs Bennett.

HORTENSE: How do you do?

EVERTON: Marcus, why yuh doan offer de young lady a seat? My dear, dis boy of mine got no manners.

> HORTENSE *gives him a look.*

Scene 22

Int. MISS MAY's *kitchen. Day.*

> *We see* WALTER *preparing the chicken. He is out of dressing-gown now.*

Shirt, cardigan, trousers and an apron. We see him seasoning a very dismal-looking bird: salt, pepper, garlic. Lots of garlic. MISS MAY *overseeing.*

MISS MAY (*seeing him go mad with the garlic*):   Walter, how much garlic yuh usin'? Yuh worse dan a Eye-talian.

WALTER: Jus' call me de 'Gal-Gal-Gallopin' Gor-may'.

MISS MAY: Doan get above y'self, Walter.

> WALTER *puts chicken in oven.*

Scene 23

Int. EVERTON's *house, dining-room. Day.*

> *They have finished their main course. We see* HORTENSE *entering with a bowl of ice-cream.*

RANJANAA: More food. Mrs Bennett, this is the best meal I've had since my mother died.

HORTENSE: Chile, yuh modder is dead?

RANJANAA: Yes. About ten months ago.

HORTENSE: Marcus, you din tell me dat.

RANJANAA: Delicious. Will you tell me how to make it?

HORTENSE: Marcus, you mus' bring Ranjanaa here more often.

EVERTON (*elbowing* RANJANAA):   Yuh in, girl, yuh in!

> *They all laugh.*

Scene 24

Int. MISS MAY's *kitchen. Day.*

> *We see* WALTER *taking chicken out of oven. It is a bit overcooked to say the least. He puts it in front of* MISS MAY.

WALTER: Voilà!

MISS MAY: Walter, I dunno what you call dis. You suppose to cook it. Not cremate it.

WALTER (*very unsure*):   It's jus' a b-b-bit brown.

MISS MAY: Jus' a bit. Anyway (*she gets up*) ah doan feel in no mood to eat.

> *She leaves the room.* WALTER *left alone. He sags. Looks very hurt.*

Scene 25

Int. EVERTON's *house. Dining-room. Day.*

MARCUS: Mother, why didn't you invite Uncle Walter to come an' have Sunday lunch with us?

HORTENSE: Why? He'd only bring dat woman along wit' 'im. Dat wife of 'is.

MARCUS: What's wrong wit' her?

    HORTENSE *just sucks her teeth.*

EVERTON (*to* MARCUS):   Apparently de police arrested Desmon' now. Slowly but surely dey mean to arrest dat whole family. It's a good thing she only got two sons. Or dey'd need a bigger police station in Thornley.

RANJANAA (*to* MARCUS):   Who is Desmond?

MARCUS: A boy who works in my father's shop. He's in trouble with the police. He an' 'is brother.

EVERTON: They were at some club an' dey were refused admission. Hardly surprisin'. Dey always look like Bill an' Ben, de Flowerpot Men. Of course, accordin' to dem it's prejudice. De doorman's a *Nazi*. An dat's jus' de nice side of 'im. But I know some *black* clubs dat wouldn't allow dem in, de way dey dress.

RANJANAA: It could be prejudice. It does happen. More than once I have been called a wog.

MARCUS: She's right, Dad. Maybe they were tellin' the truth. We ought to do something.

EVERTON: Like what?

MARCUS: We could visit that club. You an' me.

Scene 26

Int. 'The Midnight Lady'. Hallway. Night.

    FOSTER *in attendance. His face bears evidence of his fight with* DESMOND *and* ROYSTON. GIRL *selling tickets. Then* EVERTON *and* MARCUS *approach.* EVERTON *in jacket and tie.* MARCUS *in polo-neck sweater and jacket.*

FOSTER (*as he sees them approaching*):   Look at this, Batman an' Robin.

    They come closer. He bars their way.

FOSTER: Sorry, this is a members-only club.

    A beat.

MARCUS: How you know we're not members?

FOSTER: I'm partly bionic. Let's have no trouble, okay?

MARCUS: Trouble? We're not the Mafia.

FOSTER: Jus' go, John, okay?

EVERTON: How can we join your club?

FOSTER: My friend, take my word for it, there's nothing special about this club. You'd hate it. We can't even spell the word 'reggae'.

EVERTON: Reggae? Me?

MARCUS (*to* GIRL *selling tickets*):   Miss, you can't say we're not tryin'. We'd like to join yuh club. How much does membership cost?

FOSTER *puts his hand on* MARCUS's *arm.*

FOSTER (*calm for him*): I'm a reasonable man.

Pause.

MARCUS: Take yuh flickin' han's off me. Off.

Pause. FOSTER *removes his hand.*

FOSTER: Right. That's it. Out.

Pause.

EVERTON: Yuh're preventin' me from joinin' your club, dat's final, is it?
FOSTER: Yer finally got the message.
EVERTON: Den ah'm gonna sue dis club.
FOSTER: You what?
EVERTON: Ah don't fight wit' fists. I got solicitors to do my fightin' for me.

EVERTON *and* MARCUS *walk out of the club.*

Scene 27

Int. EVERTON's *shop – back room.*

EVERTON *on telephone.*

EVERTON: Hello, can ah speak to Mr Levy, tell 'im it's Everton Bennett ...
Hello, Sidney, how're you ...? An' how day boy of yours, still runnin' after
de shiksas[2] ...? Yuh think you got problems, my son's runnin' after an
Indian girl. Yes, well, anyway, listen; dere's something ah want you to do
fo' me, ah've had a bit of bother in a club called 'The Midnight Lady', an'
ah'm gonna sue them, or radder you're gonna sue dem for me.

Scene 28

Int. EVERTON's *shop. Day.*

EVERTON *at till, tending to* TWO CUSTOMERS. *Enter* FOSTER *and* MICHAEL
RENTON. RENTON: *English, owner of 'The Midnight Lady', thirties. Wide boy
made good. The* TWO CUSTOMERS *leave.*

FOSTER: That's him.
RENTON: Hello, I'm Mr Renton. I own 'The Midnight Lady'.
EVERTON: Good fo' you, but as ah tole yuh frien' here ... (*a nod in* FOSTER's
direction) I got a good solicitor. Any talkin' that needs to be done, he's de
man to see.

---

[2] *shiksas:* Yiddish for girls who are not Jewish.

FOSTER (*to* RENTON):   See. You can't reason with some of them, can you? They've only just come down from the trees.

EVERTON (*moving close to* FOSTER):   Lemme say dis once. Thornley is full uh West Indians who owe me a favour. If dey thought fo' one minute dat something, or someone, was boddern' me, dey'd be more dan happy to fix dat someone for me. An' dat's so help me God.

Pause.

RENTON: Why don't you wait in the car for me, Danny, okay?

Pause. FOSTER *exits.*

RENTON: I know it's hard to believe, but you should see him playin' with his kids, it's a sight that never fails to gladden my heart. Let me say this right away. When Danny stopped you enterin' my club, he was *not* acting on my orders. What can I say? I'm sorry. I am a friend of the coloured people. More power to all of you, I say. As for that Muhammad Ali, how he does it at his age, I'll never know. Magic. (*Suddenly serious*) Now about this writ of yours. This writ this solicitor served on us. You can't be serious.

EVERTON: My frien', many blacks have a reputation fo' not being serious, but when it comes to money, ah'm de exception dat proves de rule.

RENTON: Mr Bennett, you couldn't win a case like this, take my word for it.

EVERTON: But what about the publicity? I'm a man who owns a number of houses and you turned me away. I'm not some teenager out to cause trouble. Can you see the newspaper headlines? Reckon that'll be good for your club.

RENTON: What do you want?

EVERTON: Your Mr Foster. He had a run-in wit' two black youths some time las' week.

RENTON: So?

EVERTON: He's accusing two young men that I know – one of dem works in dis shop. Desmond and Royston Reid. Now, if Mr Foster could be persuaded to reconsider ... that perhaps it was a case of mistaken identity.

RENTON: Desmond and Royston Reid. Can't say as I know them. I'm sure Mr Foster has never seen them either. These kids, they all look alike, don't they?

EVERTON *smiles.*

Scene 29
Int. EVERTON's *shop. The following day.*

WALTER *is sweeping the shop.* EVERTON *is in the back room. Suddenly* MISS MAY, DESMOND *and* ROYSTON *descend on the shop. We hear* MAY *even before we see her.*

MAY (*off*):   Where is 'e! Godfadder!

She and her sons appear. WALTER *sighs, heavenwards.* EVERTON *comes out from back room.*

EVERTON: Who is dat? Who is dat keepin' all dat noise in my shop?

MAY: It's Wonderloaf! (*She gives him a big kiss.*)

EVERTON (*jumping back*): Dis woman is a menace!

MAY: Bless yuh, bless yuh.

EVERTON: What dam foolishness is dis?

DESMOND: I knew you would help, Godfadder.

MAY: Royston!

ROYSTON (*to* EVERTON, *hands in pockets*): Yeah, yeah, you're okay.

EVERTON (*drily*): T'anks. Ah'll come to you any time ah need a reference. Who knows, by den yuh might even have learnt to write. (*Then*) Desmon'. How come you got Walter sweepin' up? You not doing yuh job, boy.

DESMOND (*cheerfully*): Sorry, sorry, Godfadder. Yuh heard de boss. Give me the broom, Walter.

MAY: Godfadder! Godfadder!

MAY *and* ROYSTON *start to leave the shop.*

EVERTON: Hold on. May, ah'd like a quiet word wit' Royston.

She stops. A beat. She looks at EVERTON. *Pause.*

MAY: He needs it.

A beat. She exits.

EVERTON: Okay, you two come wit' me. (*To* DESMOND) You an' yuh brodder.

EVERTON *walks to the back of the shop.*

ROYSTON: What's all dis to rahtid?

DESMOND (*pulling* ROYSTON *along, roughly*): Come on.

They join EVERTON.

EVERTON: Right, you two. Get dis in yuh head. Never again. Hear me? You get arrested fo' anything serious again, an' you can forget I even exist. Cos yuh can be sure ah'll forget *you* exist. Assault is a serious crime.

ROYSTON *sighs, looks away.*

EVERTON: Royston, when ah'm talkin' to you I wan' your two eyes on me, *all de time.* Do ah make myself clear? You jus' look away again an' ah'll knock you down. Ah'm talkin' to you, understan' me?

ROYSTON: Man, you worse dan de police.

EVERTON: Dat's right. Ah'm worse dan de police. So you jus' remember dat de nex' time you think of breakin' de law. (*Then*) Let me spell it out fo' yuh. Yuh no good to yuhself or anybody when yuh in a bloody prison. Dat's de one thing dey doan tell yuh. Dey tell yuh how it's not your fault, it's society's fault, an' how de Man's[3] doin' dis to you, an' de Man's doin' dat. Well, sure dat's true. But how much comfort is dat to you when you're behin' bars? Ah'll say it one more time. Yuh no good to nobody, not even yuhself, once yuh in a prison. Wake up.

Pause.

ROYSTON: Words, man. Dem's just words. Water off my back. See yuh around ... (*he curls his lip*) ... Godfadder.

[3] *de Man*: White man, white society.

ROYSTON *starts to go.* DESMOND *catches hold of his hand.*

DESMOND: Rahtid ...!

Brother squares up in front of brother. Pause.

EVERTON (*a command*): Let 'im go, Desmon'. (*A beat*) He's yuh brodder.

Pause. DESMOND *stands aside. A beat.* ROYSTON *exits. Pause.*
TWO CUSTOMERS *enter.* EVERTON *makes an effort to pull himself together.*

EVERTON: Well, let's get on wit' it.

They move forward to serve the TWO CUSTOMERS.

SUGGESTIONS FOR WRITING AND DISCUSSION

1 *If you have read* The Street Party, *describe how themes in that play have been developed here (e.g. race prejudice and the attitude to work).*
2 *Describe what further insight you get into the characters of* The Street Party *by reading* Royston's Day.
3 *What do you learn about the character of Everton from* Royston's Day? *Sum up his philosophy of life.*
4 *Comment on the way this episode ends. What do you think the viewer/ reader is meant to conclude?*
5 *Drama is made up of the conflict between one character and another or one view and another. Sum up the conflicts that exist in* Royston's Day.
6 *Describe the character of Royston. What do you feel about him?*
7 *Describe where you think the comedy lies in* Royston's Day.
8 *Compare the characters and situations in this play with those in* Coronation Street *and* Crossroads.
9 *Write a story or a play in which someone gets into trouble with the police.*
10 *Write a story or a play in which someone takes his or her friend home to meet parents for the first time.*
11 *Write your own version, as a script or a short story, of what Royston does after this episode ends.*
12 *What do you think would be the effect of having a greater number of black programmes on television than there are at present?*
13 *Write about an incident where you have been discriminated against on racial grounds.*
14 *Write, as a script or short story, an episode involving Miss May and Walter.*
15 *Improvise your own incident where someone gets into trouble with the police (e.g. a case of mistaken identity). If possible have your characters speaking in more than one accent and at least one in dialect.*
16 *Choose one incident from the play and say how you think the use of dialect increases the viewers' enjoyment and understanding as a whole.*

JACK
ROSENTHAL

Jack Rosenthal has a Jewish
background and was born in
Manchester in 1931. He studied
English at Sheffield University.
He began writing for television
in 1961 with Episode 30 of
Coronation Street and went on
to write a further 150 episodes.
He has contributed scripts to
comedy programmes and
written situation comedies
(such as *The Dustbinmen* and
The Lovers) and plays. Among
his plays are: *Another Sunday
and Sweet F.A.*; *Ready When
You Are, Mr McGill*; *Your
Name's Not God – It's Edgar*;
Polly Put the Kettle On; *Mr Ellis
Versus the People*; *There'll
Almost Always Be an England*;
Well, Thank You; *Thursday*;
Bar Mitzvah Boy and *Spend,
Spend, Spend*. *The Evacuees*
won the International Emmy
Award, the British Academy of
Film and Television Arts Best

Play Award and the Broadcasting Press Guild Play Award in 1975.

The Evacuees is an original television play – that is, it was conceived and developed for the medium of television from the very beginning without being based on any literary source. The story is told and the characters are delineated by all the means available to a television dramatist – actors, sets, lighting, words, music obviously, but also the way one scene is placed next to another, the cutting from one scene to another, the use of close-ups, voice-over, point of view, and so on. If the story of *The Evacuees* were to be told as a novel or as a stage play, then the approach would have to be quite different and the material would have to be completely reorganized. As a simple example, it would be difficult and unsatisfactory to use the first four scenes of the play as presented here or the ideas contained in them as the opening of a novel or a stage play. They would have to be rethought.

It would be possible to make the script as written into a film rather than a television play, and the difference between the two is difficult to define. Films are likely to use a greater variety and complexity of settings, a larger number of scenes and shots, a greater diversity of camera angles, more crowd scenes and larger casts – though it is not really possible to generalize. Once, television plays were shown live with long sequences in a limited number of settings and a limited number of camera possibilities, rather like televising a stage play. Now, much greater use is made of filming and film techniques.

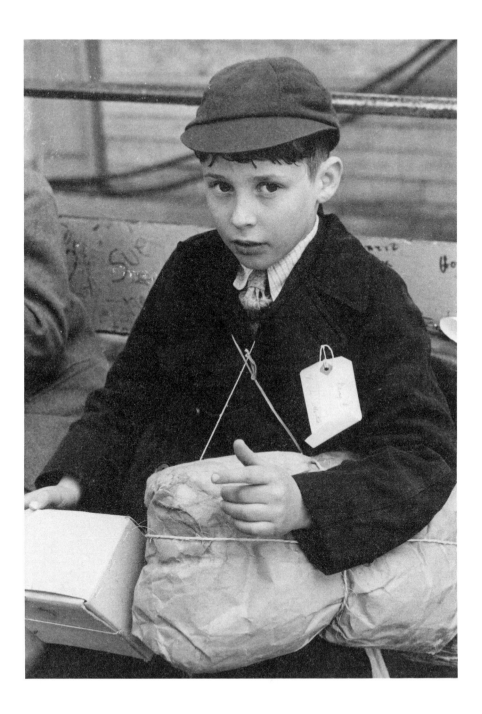

THE EVACUEES

CHARACTERS

SARAH	WORKMAN
LOUIS	FIREMAN
MRS GRAHAM	AMBULANCE MAN
DANNY	OFFICE WOMAN
NEVILLE	PHOTOGRAPHER
GRANDMA	MR GROSSFINE
ZUCKERMAN	MAN IN OVERALLS
WILHELM	'BANANA WOMAN'
MR GOLDSTONE	FIRST HOUSEWIFE
MR GRAHAM	SECOND HOUSEWIFE
PHILIP HYMAN	THIRD HOUSEWIFE
BERNARD	GANG RINGLEADER
MERTON	

Scene 1

Ext. Street 'A', Cheetham Hill, Manchester. Morning.

> *A bleak industrial street – like Derby Street – where the narrow streets of the Jewish quarter begin to widen into the big city streets of town.*
> *Caption: 'Manchester. 1 September 1939'. Fade caption on establishing an equally bleak school building, black and forbidding.*
> *Over this, and Scenes 2 and 3, we hear the voice of a teacher,* MR GOLDSTONE, *taking the roll-call in his class of nine-year-olds, and the voices of his pupils replying.*

MR GOLDSTONE (*V.O.*):[1] Aaron.
AARON (*V.O.*): Present, Sir.
MR GOLDSTONE (*V.O.*): Abrahams.
ABRAHAMS (*V.O.*): Yes, Sir.
MR GOLDSTONE (*V.O.*): Bergman.
BERGMAN (*V.O.*): Yes, Sir.
MR GOLDSTONE (*V.O.*): Bloom.

Scene 2

Ext. Street 'A', Cheetham Hill. Morning.

> *An elderly woman –* GRANDMA *– is shuffling speedily down the street. Slightly dotty at the best of times, she's now muttering to herself – agitatedly and tearfully. From time to time she explodes into a sudden angry outburst, then subsides again with a fatalistic shrug of resignation. She's carrying a small brown paper bag. Over this, the roll-call continues.*

BLOOM (*V.O.*): Present, Sir.
MR GOLDSTONE (*V.O.*): Cohen J.
COHEN J. (*V.O.*): Yes, Sir.
MR GOLDSTONE (*V.O.*): Cohen L.
COHEN L. (*V.O.*): Yes, Sir.
MR GOLDSTONE (*V.O.*): Cohen S. (*No reply*) Cohen S.
ZUCKERMAN (*V.O.*): Please, Sir, his mam says to tell you he's feeling bilious.
MR GOLDSTONE (*V.O.*): Thank you, Zuckerman.
ZUCKERMAN (*V.O.*): He's probably up to his ears in Kruschen Salts.[2]
MR GOLDSTONE (*V.O.*): Shut up, Zuckerman.
ZUCKERMAN (*V.O.*): Yes, Sir.
MR GOLDSTONE (*V.O.*): Davidson.

---

[1] V.O.: voice-over.
[2] *Kruschen Salts*: health salts.

Scene 3
Ext. School building.

With lip trembling Jewishly, GRANDMA *makes her way towards the entrance of the school, and goes in. Over this, the roll-call continues.*

DAVIDSON (*V.O.*):   Present, Sir.
MR GOLDSTONE (*V.O.*):   Gluckman.
GLUCKMAN (*V.O.*):   Yes, Sir.
MR GOLDSTONE (*V.O.*):   Jacobs.
JACOBS (*V.O.*):   Yes, Sir.
MR GOLDSTONE (*V.O.*):   Kestler.
KESTLER (*V.O.*):   Present, Sir.
MR GOLDSTONE (*V.O.*):   Miller.
DANNY (*V.O.*):   Yes, Sir.

Scene 4
Int. Classroom. Morning.

*About twenty boys are seated at their desks. They're all about nine years old and wearing well-worn schoolcaps and raincoats or overcoats. (One or two are coatless and rather more ragged than the rest.) They all have gas-mask cases slung round their shoulders and their names on cardboard labels pinned to their lapels. (*ZUCKERMAN *has no gas-mask case.) A youngish teacher – MR* GOLDSTONE *– is still taking the roll-call from his register. The last few names in the roll-call are confirmed by shouts from boys dotted at random round the class.*

MR GOLDSTONE: Rabinowitz.
RABINOWITZ: Present, Sir.
MR GOLDSTONE: Schwarz. All right, Schwarz. Tushner.
TUSHNER: Yes, Sir.
MR GOLDSTONE: Wise.
WISE: Yes, Sir.
MR GOLDSTONE: Weisberg.
WEISBERG: Yes, Sir.
MR GOLDSTONE: Winkler.
WINKLER: Yes, Sir.
MR GOLDSTONE: Zuckerman.
ZUCKERMAN: Present and correct, Sir!
MR GOLDSTONE: Where's your gas-mask, Zuckerman?
ZUCKERMAN: Please, Sir, I don't know.
MR GOLDSTONE: *Why* don't you know?
ZUCKERMAN: I don't know, Sir.
MR GOLDSTONE: You're a blockhead, Zuckerman. What are you?
ZUCKERMAN: Please, Sir, a blockhead.

The rest of the class titters.

MR GOLDSTONE: Silence!

They promptly fall silent. DANNY *continues laughing for a moment, after the others have stopped. A look from* MR GOLDSTONE *silences him.*

MR GOLDSTONE: Now, then. When the bell goes, we all leave the classroom *quietly*, and in orderly *fashion*, and walk ... and when I say walk I mean walk ... in single file down to the playground.

He looks towards a thin, serious-faced boy slightly older than the rest, with closely cropped hair. This is WILHELM SCHWARZ, *an Austrian refugee. He wears indoor clothes and has no gas-mask. (Throughout the entire play, he wears a yarmulka.[3])*

MR GOLDSTONE: Except you of course, Schwarz. (WILHELM *nods.*) Just carry on with your reading exercises, while we're away. (WILHELM *nods.* MR GOLDSTONE *resumes his instructions to the rest of the class.*)
Once in the playground, we line up – in *order* – with the rest of the school. Standard One next to the fire escape, then Standard Two, then you lot, then Standard Four and so on. (*There's a sudden yelp of pain from one of the boys.*) Yes, Weisberg?

WEISBERG: Please, Sir, someone threw a bean-bag at me! (*He holds the bean-bag as evidence.*)

MR GOLDSTONE (*not looking at* ZUCKERMAN): Zuckerman, stop throwing bean-bags at Weisberg.

ZUCKERMAN (*injured innocence*): Please, Sir, I never, honest! (MR GOLDSTONE *ignores him and resumes his instructions to the class.*)

MR GOLDSTONE: Once lined up, the whole school – apart from Schwarz here and a few others – will then go *quietly* – and *how* – Zuckerman?

ZUCKERMAN: In orderly fashion, Sir.

MR GOLDSTONE: In orderly fashion – to Cheetham Hill Road, where special trams will be waiting to take us to Victoria Station. We'll get off, line up in single file, then get on again, and come back to school – where Zuckerman will no doubt continue his education by looking at pictures of Desperate Dan eating cow-pie.

ZUCKERMAN *hastily and guiltily shuts the pages of the comic he's been surreptitiously trying to read. The others laugh. The laughter suddenly dies as the door bursts open. Standing in the doorway is* GRANDMA – *looking feverishly round the class with tear-filled eyes. Everyone stares at her uncomprehendingly.*

MR GOLDSTONE (*blankly*): Good morning, Mrs ... er ... Mrs Mendelberg ...

GRANDMA (*absently*): 'Miller.'

---

[3] *yarmulka*: small caplet worn by a religious Jew.

MR GOLDSTONE: Sorry ... 'Miller' ... Um, what exactly ...?

GRANDMA: Where's my ... (*She scans the room and finally catches sight of her grandson,* DANNY, *and cries tragically*) – Danny!! (DANNY *sits, embarrassed and perplexed, as she does her shuffling sprint over to him, moaning heartbrokenly.*) Bubbele![4] Little bubbele! They want they should take you away – a fire on their kishkes![5]

>   DANNY, *to his horror, realizes that any second now his* GRANDMA *is going to clutch his head to her breast in front of the entire class. He's right.* GRANDMA *holds his head against her and rocks to and fro.*

GRANDMA: My shaney little tateleh![6] Let them take my right arm – that they can have, take, gezuntereit![7] (DANNY *silently prays for death.*)

MR GOLDSTONE: Mrs Miller, no one's taking your grandson away.

>   GRANDMA *ignores him.*

GRANDMA (*to* DANNY):   Tateleh ... trains, evacuations – who needs? Stay, darling, be happy. (*To* MR GOLDSTONE *accusingly*) A *baby*, he is!

MR GOLDSTONE (*patiently*):   Mrs Miller. It's a *practice*. Evacuation *practice*. We're going to the station and back. He'll be away an *hour*. Three-quarters.

>   *None of which* GRANDMA *has listened to. She sobs into* DANNY's *hair a moment, then turns on* MR GOLDSTONE *again, bitterly.*

GRANDMA: And you a teacher. Nice. A clever man. Letters behind your name.

>   *She nods sadly, ironically, at the enormity of his wickedness, and hugs* DANNY's *head closer to her breast.* DANNY *hears the tittering of his classmates and shuts his eyes.*

GRANDMA: Every Friday, a lifetime, I chop and fry gefilte fish. You should taste my fish. My fish I could win medals for at the Midland Hotel. Only *this* Friday, how? With *tears*, eppas?[8] And not from the onions – from the *heart*. A baby they take – may they lig in dred.[9] A baby goes to the wars – that's a teacher? That's in library books?

MR GOLDSTONE (*wearily*):   Mrs Miller, there *is* no war. It's a practice in *case* there's a war. There's not even going to be a war. And if there *is* it'll be over by Christmas.

>   GRANDMA *looks at him – slowly beginning to understand the situation.*

GRANDMA: Is a practice?

---

[4] *bubbele*: darling, dear child.
[5] *kishkes*: innards, guts.
[6] *my shaney little tateleh*: my pretty little boy.
[7] *gezuntereit*: go in health.
[8] *eppas*: maybe.
[9] *lig in dred*: lie in fear.

MR GOLDSTONE: That's all.
GRANDMA: He'll be home tonight, please God?
MR GOLDSTONE: This afternoon.

A pause. GRANDMA *slowly releases* DANNY's *head.*

GRANDMA: His mother said . . . (*Shrugs*) Ah! . . . people talk too quick these days. I'll go, gezuntereit. (*Sharply to* DANNY) Sit nice, like a mensch.[10] (DANNY *sits up correctly.*) Put your cap straight. (*She straightens it for him.*) Better. (*Pause, then quietly*) I'd made you a piece fried fish for the travelling. (*She plonks the brown paper bag on his desk and exits.*)

Scene 5
Ext. Street 'B', Cheetham Hill. Early evening.

A dingy street in the heart of the Jewish quarter. DANNY *and his twelve-year-old brother,* NEVILLE, *are playing marbles with two or three other kids in the road and gutter. One of the boys is called* ALEC. *A few yards away, watching them, is* WILHELM, *leaning against a wall, hands in pockets. Two girls are playing with whips and tops nearby. The boys play for a moment, rowdily, then* NEVILLE *notices* WILHELM.

NEVILLE: Want a game? (WILHELM *shakes his head.*) Did you play alleys in Austria?

WILHELM *shrugs to indicate he doesn't know. An older boy,* MERTON, *about fifteen years old, passes, wearing ordinary clothes apart from heavy football boots and his trousers tucked into his socks. He bounces an old leather football in front of him as he walks.* DANNY *watches his approach with hero-worshipping eyes.*

NEVILLE: Hello, Merton.
MERTON (*cool*):   Howdo.
DANNY: Hello, Merton.
MERTON (*amiably*):   Tiddler.

He continues on his way. DANNY *watches.*

DANNY: He's one of the best dribblers in England, isn't he, Merton?
NEVILLE: He's okay.
DANNY: He'll play for Wolves when he's grown up. Any money.
ALEC: Why the Wolves?
DANNY: Any money, he will. It's irrelevant.
ALEC: Why not City or the Rags?
NEVILLE: He supports the Wolves, our kid. He likes the name.

---

[10] *like a mensch*: like a proper man.

ALEC: He's barmy.

DANNY: Why am I?

ALEC: Wolves can't play for toffee.

NEVILLE (*to* DANNY):   Hit him.

DANNY (*a touch scared*):   I will in a minute.

ALEC: Yeah? You and whose army?

DANNY: Shurrup, you!

ALEC: What if I don't?

NEVILLE (*to* DANNY):   Bash his head in.

DANNY (*evasively*):   Look, I thought we was playing alleys!

ALEC: You're scared.

DANNY: Who is?

ALEC: You is.

NEVILLE *grabs* ALEC *and pins him to the ground, then turns to* DANNY.

NEVILLE: Go on, our kid! Now! Thump him!

DANNY (*evasively*):   I might. I might not.

NEVILLE *releases* ALEC.

NEVILLE: It's all right, Alec, he wouldn't. (*Amused*) Going to be a rabbi,[11] aren't you, Danny? (*He laughs.*)

DANNY *promptly hurls himself at* NEVILLE. NEVILLE *trots off up the street, laughing and handing off* DANNY, *who's pursuing him – raining ineffectual punches.*

NEVILLE (*while dodging*):   What sort of job's that for a Yiddishe[12] boy?

Scene 6

Int. The Millers' living-room. Continuous in time.

The house and furniture are very working class. Open on GRANDMA *lighting the two Sabbath candles and saying the prayer.* SARAH – DANNY *and* NEVILLE's *mother – is laying the table for dinner. She's a blonde.* LOUIS – *the boys' father – is polishing his boots by the fire.*

GRANDMA: Boruch atto adonai Elohanu melech ho-oulom. Asher kidashonu b'mitzvousov. Votzeevonu. L'chadlik nair shel-shabbos.[13]

She starts to light the candles. SARAH *is placing a big bowl of soup on to the table.*

---

[11] *rabbi*: Jewish teacher, religious leader.

[12] *Yiddishe*: Jewish.

[13] *Boruch ... shel-shabbos*: Jewish prayer, repeated as the candles are lit.

SARAH (*to* LOUIS):   Ever since I got home from work ... Sticking her finger in the soup, sucking it, saying 'It needs more salt'. Then sticking it back in again ...

GRANDMA (*to* SARAH *and* LOUIS, *as she finishes lighting the candles*):   Good shabbos.[14]

LOUIS *hands* SARAH *his pay-packet*.

LOUIS: Fruits of my labours.

SARAH (*looking at the amount on the back of the packet*):   Two pound ten ...??

GRANDMA: I said 'Good shabbos'.

LOUIS: Things are slack everywhere. They're worried there'll be a war ... (*To* GRANDMA) Good shabbos.

SARAH: How do we manage on two pound ten?

LOUIS: Two pound seven and six. I owed half a dollar union money.

GRANDMA (*pointedly to* SARAH):   I said 'Good shabbos'.

SARAH: I know. (*She sighs.*) Good shabbos. I'll get the kids in.

She starts to exit to the hall. GRANDMA *dips her finger into the soup, sucks it and grimaces.*

GRANDMA (*to* LOUIS):   It needed more salt ...

SARAH (*shouting from the door*):   It *got* more salt!

GRANDMA, *chastened, dips her finger in again and sucks it.*

GRANDMA: Mmmm! (*Appreciatively*) Believe me, I can tell! (*To* LOUIS) Beautiful!

Scene 7

Ext. Street 'B', Cheetham Hill. Continuous in time.

NEVILLE *still teasingly avoiding* DANNY's *flailing fists.* SARAH *appears at the doorway, and calls.*

SARAH: Danny! Neville! Dinner!

NEVILLE: In a sec.

SARAH: Now!

DANNY: Our kid's got to win his blood-alley back!

SARAH: Are you asking for a good hiding, the pair of you?

NEVILLE *and* DANNY *start off back to the house and pass a couple of workmen who are cutting iron railings from outside the houses and loading them on to a horse and cart.*

---

[14] *shabbos*: Sabbath. Begins just before sunset on Fridays.

DANNY: Where are they taking the railings?

WORKMAN: For munitions. In case war breaks out.

DANNY: Railings???

NEVILLE calls to WILHELM who's still watching.

NEVILLE: We're going in now.

WILHELM nods and shrugs. NEVILLE picks up the marbles.

NEVILLE: Ta, ra.

WILHELM shyly nods acknowledgement and wanders off in the opposite direction.

DANNY: He gives me the creeps, Wilhelm ...

He and NEVILLE start off towards their house.

SARAH (*calling from the door*):   Come on! You'll have it dark!

DANNY turns and calls back to the workman.

DANNY: Mr Goldstone at school says there isn't going to *be* no war!

They walk on till they reach the door.

SARAH: Look at your knees! Like baitsommer![15]

DANNY and NEVILLE automatically guard their heads with their arms as they dash past their mother's threatening raised hand and into the hall. The threat isn't carried out. SARAH follows them in and closes the door behind herself.

Scene 8
Int. Mr Grossfine's shop. Day.

MR GROSSFINE is serving DANNY with the family's Sunday-morning bagels.[16]

Scene 9
Ext. School building. Day.

Over Scenes 8 and 9, we hear the voice of NEVILLE CHAMBERLAIN in his radio broadcast of 3 September 1939, announcing the declaration of war.

---

[15] *Like baitsommer*: Like a hooligan's.

[16] *bagel*: round loaf of bread or roll, traditional Jewish Sunday-morning breakfast.

CHAMBERLAIN (*V.O.*):   This morning, the British Ambassador in Berlin hand-
ed the German Government a note, stating that unless we heard from them
by eleven o'clock, that they were prepared to withdraw their troops from
Poland, a state of war would exist between us. I have to tell you now that no
such undertaking has been received, and that consequently this country is
at war with Germany.

*Overlay the end of the above on to the opening of Scene 10, mixing the
sound into the beginning of* MR GOLDSTONE's *roll-call.*

Scene 10

Int. Classroom. Morning.

*The class is seated as before, except that now each boy has a labelled
haversack or suitcase on top of his desk. (All except* WILHELM, *who has no
coat or case.)* MR GOLDSTONE *stands before them – in hat and coat – holding
a clipboard of papers detailing evacuation procedure. Everyone is now
serious – some of the boys pale and apprehensive. Solemn. As opposed to
his earlier scenes,* MR GOLDSTONE *is rather gravely brisk and purposeful.
He's calling the roll from the register.*

MR GOLDSTONE: Weisberg.

WEISBERG: Present.

MR GOLDSTONE: Winkler.

WINKLER: Present.

MR GOLDSTONE: Zuckerman.

ZUCKERMAN: Present.

MR GOLDSTONE: Got your gas-mask, Zuckerman?

ZUCKERMAN: Yes, Sir.

MR GOLDSTONE: Now, pay attention, all of you. When the bell goes, into the
playground. Line up next to Standard Two. Then – tram, then – railway
station. Parents will see you off at the platform . . . Any brothers from other
Standards will travel with you. When we get to Blackpool, you'll all be
issued with – given, that is – a tin of corned beef. Then we'll set off and try
and find . . . get you fixed up with foster-parents in either Blackpool or St
Anne's. Right. Stand up. (*They all stand up, except* WILHELM. MR GOLDSTONE
notices him.) Oh. Sorry, Schwarz. You may as well go home now. Tomorrow morning, go to Mr Davidson's class. You'll all be in the same class – all
those not being evacuated. All right? (WILHELM *nods.*) And I'll see you soon
and the Dead-End kids here'll see you as soon as we've won the war. Off
you go, lad.

WILHELM *makes his way to the door. He glances awkwardly at the row of
boys as he goes. He looks at* DANNY. DANNY *nods and smiles briefly.* WILHELM
stiffly makes to shake DANNY's *hand – but* DANNY *doesn't understand what*

he's expected to do. WILHELM *embarrassedly withdraws his hand.* ZUCKER-MAN *sniggers.* WILHELM *exits. The school bell abruptly rings.*

MR GOLDSTONE: All got your luggage? (*The boys heave their haversacks and cases.*) Right, now first row lead off and – oh! one more thing. Some of you – *most* of you – will be going to people who aren't Jewish. The food won't be kosher.[17] Now, it doesn't matter. It isn't a sin. There's a war on. Try and remember to put your tzizit[18] on every morning. Now, first row – quietly . . . (*The first row starts to file towards the door.*)

Scene 11
Ext. Railway carriage. Victoria Station. Morning.

    SARAH, DANNY *and* NEVILLE – *amid a crush of other mothers and children – struggling to board the train. Much noise, bustle and chaos.*

Scene 12
Int. Railway carriage. Victoria Station. Morning.

    A chaos of bustling activity. A few boys – including DANNY *and* NEVILLE – *are organizing themselves for the journey. There's a tremendous hubbub of noise – mostly caused by several mothers helping their sons get their haversacks on to the luggage racks and straightening their dishevelled caps, ties and socks.* SARAH *is attending to* DANNY *and* NEVILLE. *Throughout the scene she's very close to tears – but trying to hide it, not altogether successfully, beneath a determined calmness and conviviality.*

SARAH: And I'll get your address from Mr Goldstone first thing in the morning – and I'll be over to see you Saturday afternoon. Yes? So it's not long, is it? Till Saturday?

DANNY (*quietly*):   How long will you stay?

SARAH: Till Sunday night. A whole day and a half.

NEVILLE: When will you come again?

SARAH: Every two or three weeks. Month at the most. When I can afford. (*To cover her emotion, she busies herself with their appearance – including spitting on her hanky then rubbing their faces with it. Which is something kids don't like – it hurts more than you think.*) And I'll write letters. And you will. It'll be like a holiday.

DANNY: Mam, I don't think I want to go, Mam.

    We hear whistles from the guard on the platform.

---

[17] *kosher*: fulfilling the requirements of Jewish dietary law.
[18] *tzizit*: fringes at the corners of the prayer shawl.

SARAH: And be good boys to your new ... to the people that take you in, and...

DANNY: I'm fed up being evacuated, I hate it.

GRANDMA's *face suddenly becomes visible through the open window of the carriage.*

GRANDMA: You're such an expert – what you hate, what you don't hate! Blackpool's like the seaside.

NEVILLE: It *is* the seaside!

GRANDMA (*to* DANNY):   See! Listen to your brother.

SARAH: Now, you will write? Tonight? As soon as you've—

GRANDMA: Sarah – let them go, gezuntereit. (*Both women, tears very imminent, look at the two boys.*) Cheeky little chazars[19] – it'll be a holiday *without* them, believe me!

SARAH *opens the door and gets out on to the platform, turning her head away so that the boys can't see her distress.* GRANDMA *takes the opportunity to pass a brown paper bag through the window to the boys, surreptitiously.*

GRANDMA: A little chopped liver for the travelling ...

Scene 13
Ext. Platform.

SARAH *catches* GRANDMA *handing over the paper bag.*

SARAH: You've never gone and—

GRANDMA: Come on, Sarah. God's good. It's better. Away from the bombs.

Scene 14
Int. Railway carriage.

DANNY *and* NEVILLE *sit looking out at* SARAH *and* GRANDMA. NEVILLE *holds the paper bag. The noise and bustle have dissipated. Suddenly, sharply, we hear the guard's whistle. The train moves off.*

Scene 15
Ext. Platform.

SARAH *and* GRANDMA *stand and watch the train begin to pull away and gather speed. They turn and start to walk back down the platform.*

---

[19] *chazars*: pigs.

Scene 16
Ext. Promenade. Blackpool.

> DANNY's *class, led by* MR GOLDSTONE, *walk in profile along the promenade then turn inland.*

Scene 17
Ext. Blackpool, street 'A'. Afternoon.

> *Coming up the street – away from the promenade (indicated, perhaps, by a promenade 'pagoda' shelter) is most of* DANNY's *class, led by* MR GOLDSTONE, *and including* NEVILLE. *They walk up the residential street, in a crocodile, each boy carrying a tin of corned beef, as well as his case (or haversack) and gas-mask case. Some of them are fitfully singing 'Ten Green Bottles' or 'Michael Finnegan'.* ZUCKERMAN *is wearing his gas-mask.*

Scene 18
Ext. Blackpool, street 'B'.

> *The crocodile of boys walk along,* ZUCKERMAN *still wearing his gas-mask. An air-raid siren begins to wail. The boys look up at the sky, apprehensively. The singing stops.*

MR GOLDSTONE: It's not an air-raid. They're just trying the sirens out. They do it every afternoon. It's a practice.

NEVILLE (*to* DANNY):   We've heard *that* one before.

DANNY: Yes, he can tell that to the marines, can't he? (*Hoping for appreciation.*) I said he can tell that to the marines, didn't I?

> *The crocodile comes to a halt, while* MR GOLDSTONE *enters a garden gate and starts up the path to a house. At the window of the neighbouring house, a woman's face appears at the parted curtain, looks horrified at the boys, and disappears again, as the curtains are closed.* MR GOLDSTONE *rings the doorbell of her neighbour.*

MR GOLDSTONE (*without looking round*):   Take it off, Zuckerman.

> ZUCKERMAN *takes off his gas-mask. The door opens and a young* HOUSEWIFE *appears. She takes in the scene, suspiciously.*

MR GOLDSTONE: Good afternoon, madam. My name is Mr Goldstone. I'm a teacher from ...

FIRST HOUSEWIFE (*hastily*):   I can't take no evacuees!

MR GOLDSTONE: Oh.

FIRST HOUSEWIFE (*guiltily*):   I'd like to. Only ... um ... (*She tries to think of an excuse.*) Only I have this invalid father. Sorry.

MR GOLDSTONE *smiles his acknowledgement. She closes the door, and he returns to his charges. They start to tramp off to the next house.*

DANNY: I hate Her Hitler. (*'Her' mispronounced as written.*)
NEVILLE (*correcting him*):   Herr Hitler.
DANNY: What?
NEVILLE: It's 'Herr' not 'Her'.
DANNY (*defeated*):   Sometimes it's Her.
NEVILLE: Never.
DANNY: It can be. It's irrelevant.

Cut to MR GOLDSTONE *at the next door, talking to* SECOND HOUSEWIFE.

SECOND HOUSEWIFE: Sorry, I only wish I could. (*Thinks for a moment.*) Only I have three of my own, you see. Well, four, really.
MR GOLDSTONE: Three or four?
SECOND HOUSEWIFE: Four. All told. It wouldn't be doing right by them.
MR GOLDSTONE: Thank you, madam. Good day.
SECOND HOUSEWIFE: Not at all. Pleasure to be of help. (*She closes the door.*)

Scene 19
Ext. Blackpool, street 'C'.

A couple of hours later. The crocodile is now somewhat shorter – and much more weary. The boys trudge along either dragging their cases or bent double by their haversacks – still clutching their tins of corned beef. Cut to MR GOLDSTONE *talking to* THIRD HOUSEWIFE *on her doorstep.*

THIRD HOUSEWIFE (*surveying the boys doubtfully*):   Are they clean?
MR GOLDSTONE (*wearily*):   Oh, yes, madam. We have to evacuate the cleanest first, by Act of Parliament.
THIRD HOUSEWIFE: What?
MR GOLDSTONE: They're all very clean.
THIRD HOUSEWIFE: Go on, then. I'll try one.
MR GOLDSTONE: Thank you, madam. Which?

She stands, surveying the boys – like a cattle market. The boys stand looking back at her – some thrusting their chests and faces forward hoping to be chosen, others too tired and past caring. ZUCKERMAN *pulls his tongue at her.*

THIRD HOUSEWIFE: That one. (*She points to* NEVILLE.)
MR GOLDSTONE: Sorry. He's one of a pair.
THIRD HOUSEWIFE: Eh?
MR GOLDSTONE: He's with his brother. We try not to separate brothers.
THIRD HOUSEWIFE: I can't take *two* ...
MR GOLDSTONE: Can I interest you in one of the others perhaps?

THIRD HOUSEWIFE: He'll do.

She points at WINKLER. MR GOLDSTONE *pushes* WINKLER *to her and gives them both thick sheaves of paper bearing typed instructions and advice.*

MR GOLDSTONE: Say hello to the lady.

WINKLER: Hello.

MR GOLDSTONE (*while writing down the woman's address on his clipboard*):   This is Cyril Winkler.

THIRD HOUSEWIFE (*to* WINKLER):   That's a funny name, isn't it?

MR GOLDSTONE: Say yes.

WINKLER: Yes.

THIRD HOUSEWIFE (*pulling* WINKLER'*s shirt collar down slightly*):   Got a tide-mark as well, haven't you? (*She ushers him in and closes the door.*)

Scene 20
Ext. Blackpool, street 'D'. Dusk.

All that's left of the crocodile is MR GOLDSTONE, DANNY, NEVILLE *and* ZUCKERMAN. *All desperately weary, hungry and footsore. The three boys are sitting on their haversacks on the pavement, while* MR GOLDSTONE *is negotiating – with a middle-aged housewife,* MRS GRAHAM, *at her doorway.*

DANNY: I think being evacuated stinks.

ZUCKERMAN: Wilhelm Schwarz had more sense.

NEVILLE: You barm-pot! He's got foster-parents already, in Manchester!

DANNY: They said he's done enough running, Mr Goldstone said. That's why they wouldn't let him come.

ZUCKERMAN: What if the Germans get him, though? They shot his real mam and dad in Austria, didn't they?

DANNY: Czechoslovakia.

ZUCKERMAN: Austria.

DANNY: Czechoslovakia, wasn't it, our kid?

NEVILLE: No, Austria.

DANNY (*defeated*):   I meant Austria, clever! (*Pause*) The Czechoslovakian part.

A tired pause.

ZUCKERMAN: Why doesn't Wilhelm never talk? He never ever says anything. Not even at playtime even.

Another weary silence.

DANNY: Being evacuated's the worst thing in the world. It's worse than being buried up to your neck by Fuzzy-Wuzzies in the desert so's the ants get you.

ZUCKERMAN: What's next worse?

DANNY: There isn't one.

They all think for a moment.

ZUCKERMAN: What about if the Clay Men in *Flash Gordon* get you?

MR GOLDSTONE *calls from the doorway.*

MR GOLDSTONE: The Miller Boys! Come here!

DANNY *and* NEVILLE *jerk an apprehensive look to the doorway.*

MR GOLDSTONE: This is Mrs Graham. She's taking you.
NEVILLE (*picking up his haversack*):   Ta, ra, Zuckie.
DANNY (*picking up his haversack*):   See you tomorrow.
ZUCKERMAN: I bet she's a witch. Any money.

NEVILLE *takes* DANNY's *haversack from him, so that he can hold his brother's hand as they go up the path to the doorway.* MR GOLDSTONE *gives them their papers.*
Cut back to ZUCKERMAN, *sitting on his haversack, waiting.* MR GOLDSTONE *joins him.*

MR GOLDSTONE (*sighing wearily*):   Come on, Hopalong Cassidy.

ZUCKERMAN *gets up, hoists up his haversack, and they start tramping off together down the street.*

ZUCKERMAN: There's no houses *left*.
MR GOLDSTONE: There's thousands.

They walk on.

ZUCKERMAN: Please, Sir, can I go back to Manchester?
MR GOLDSTONE: No.

He strides on. ZUCKERMAN *trundles along behind him.*

ZUCKERMAN: I've got a headache in my leg.

Scene 21
Int. Mrs Graham's hallway.

DANNY *and* NEVILLE *stand in the hall, their caps on their heads, their luggage at their feet. They stand for a moment or two, looking at each other, nonplussed.*

DANNY: She's scrammed!
NEVILLE: She went up the dancers.
DANNY: What for?
NEVILLE: *I* don't know!
DANNY: Has she gone to bed?

They stand there. Small. Lonely. The bathroom door at the top of the stairs opens, we hear the sound of running water. MRS GRAHAM *appears at the bathroom door.*

MRS GRAHAM: Come along, children. A nice hot bath.
NEVILLE: We had a bath on Sunday.
MRS GRAHAM: Upstairs, please, like big boys.

She goes back inside. They start upstairs.

Scene 22
Int. Mrs Graham's lounge/dining-room. Evening.

The house and furniture are comfortably middle-class. MRS GRAHAM *is preparing the table for tea.* MR GRAHAM *is in an armchair listening to Hitler giving a speech – punctuated by a chorus of thousands shouting 'Sieg Heil!' on the wireless. From time to time* MR GRAHAM *shakes his head sadly and sighs.* DANNY *and* NEVILLE *enter from upstairs, scrubbed clean after their exhausting day, wearing identical Fair Isle pullovers, and their school caps.* DANNY *stops dead on hearing Hitler's voice – and on seeing* MR GRAHAM *listening to it. He at once suspects him of being a German spy. He glances at* NEVILLE, *who understands but dismisses the theory with an impatient shake of the head.* MRS GRAHAM *looks at them.*

MRS GRAHAM: Oh! No caps, children! Not indoors.
NEVILLE: We've always worn them.
MRS GRAHAM: I don't think so. (*She takes their caps off.*)
MRS GRAHAM: To the table, children. (*To* MR GRAHAM) Tea, dear?
MR GRAHAM: Attagirl!

He switches the wireless off, makes his way to the table and sits down. MRS GRAHAM *also sits down – in the only remaining chair. The two boys look blankly at the table, wondering where they're supposed to sit. Two plates have been laid for them – each bearing one cold sausage – but no chairs.* MR GRAHAM *bows his head in prayer.* MRS GRAHAM *likewise. The two boys stand at the table facing their plate of cold sausage.*

MR GRAHAM: For what we're about to receive, may the Lord make us truly thankful. Amen. (*He digs into his meal.*)
MRS GRAHAM: Amen. (*To the boys*) 'Amen'.
NEVILLE: Amen.
MRS GRAHAM: Danny?
DANNY: Amen – what is it?
MRS GRAHAM: 'What is it, Mrs Graham?'
DANNY (*confused*):   What? (*Looks down at the sausage.*)
MRS GRAHAM: Silly lad. It's a sausage.
NEVILLE (*to* MRS GRAHAM):   Shall we stand here?
MRS GRAHAM: You boys like football?

DANNY: Yes.

MRS GRAHAM: 'Yes, Mrs Graham.'

NEVILLE (*to* DANNY):   You've to say 'Mrs Graham' at the end of the sentence. (*To* MR GRAHAM) Sometimes, Mr Graham.

MR GRAHAM: I watch Blackpool now and then. Top of the first division. Saw them wallop the Wolves on Saturday. (*Which doesn't please* DANNY.) Two-one. Jock Dodds got both.

DANNY: I don't like cold sausage, Mrs Graham.

MRS GRAHAM: Of course you do! It's real pork.

> DANNY *and* NEVILLE *exchange an immediate frantic glance of panic. Real pork is the biggest crisis they've ever had to face.*

NEVILLE: Is there anything else instead, Mrs Graham?

MRS GRAHAM (*putting down her knife and fork*):   Neville. One thing I shall not entertain. And that's impertinence. Mr Graham and I like little boys who are grateful for being taken off the streets and given a home. (*She continues eating.*)

NEVILLE: Could we have the corned beef we brought – do you think – Mrs Graham?

MRS GRAHAM: No. That stays in the larder for when there's a shortage.

DANNY: We've never had pork sausage, Mrs Graham. We're not allowed it.

MR GRAHAM (*with consummate wisdom*):   How do you know you don't like it, then, eh? Mmmmm? Can't answer that one, can you? Eh, boys? Blinded by science, eh?

MRS GRAHAM (*to the boys, annoyed*):   Just don't know there's a war *on*, do you?

> MR *and* MRS GRAHAM *continue eating their meal.* DANNY *and* NEVILLE *look at each other.* NEVILLE *realizes he has to take the lead and make a decision. He struggles through a little crisis of conscience, then cuts a small piece of his sausage – whispers a short Hebrew prayer to himself – hand on head – and eats.* DANNY *watches. Accepts the decision and puts his hand on his head to whisper the Hebrew prayer.* MRS GRAHAM *glances at him. He pretends he's scratching his head, then drops his hand and eats.*

Scene 23

Int. The Millers' living-room. Evening.

> *Open on* DANNY's *and* NEVILLE's *empty chairs at the table.* GRANDMA, SARAH *and* LOUIS *are seated in their chairs at the table, having their evening meal. They eat in unaccustomed silence, each of them upset at the boys' absence ... and each aware of what the others are feeling.*

GRANDMA: So have you both gone stumm[20] or something? Suddenly no one talks all of a sudden!

---

[20] *stumm*: dumb.

SARAH *tries to think of something to talk about.*

SARAH (*gently*):   Is the soup salty enough for you? (*No response*) We'll go round Hightown tomorrow, eh? Get some blackout curtains.

No response. SARAH *racks her brains for another topic of conversation.*

SARAH: Louis starts fire-watching next week, don't you, Louis? (*Pause*) Watching for fires. (*Pause*) Two nights a week. In case there's –
GRANDMA: Sarah, Yachny-divossy,[21] do me a favour, stop talking. Eh? Thank you.

Scene 24
Int. The boys' bedroom. Night.

DANNY *and* NEVILLE *are lying back to back in bed – both tired but awake. Faintly, from downstairs, we hear on the wireless 'Monday Night at 8 o'Clock'. The boys are silent for a few moments. Looking into space, mulling over the events of the day.*

DANNY: If he isn't a spy, why was he listening to Her Hitler?
NEVILLE: *Herr* Hitler. He isn't. Go to sleep.
DANNY: Your big fat elbow's only sticking in my ribs. (NEVILLE *shifts position slightly. Tears imminent*) Neville ...
NEVILLE: Go to sleep.
DANNY: It'll be over by Christmas, won't it? Any money?
NEVILLE: 'Course.
DANNY: We'll write to Mam tomorrow. (*Pause*) Railings can't do much against *tanks*. You can only make spears out of railings.

A long pause. They seem to be settling down to sleep. We hear DANNY *quietly sobbing to himself.* NEVILLE *listens to him – fighting back his own tears.*

NEVILLE: We'll be all right. (DANNY *continues sobbing.*) Sssshhh. (DANNY *continues sobbing.* NEVILLE *gets up on one elbow and belts his brother across the head.*) Now, shurrup!!

DANNY *quietens down. A pause.*

DANNY: I forgot to say my prayers.
NEVILLE: Do you want another good hiding?

DANNY *whispers his prayers to himself.*

DANNY: Boruch atto adonai Elohanu melech ho'oulom. Hamapeel chevlai ... er ... (*He's lost. He tries again.*) Hamapeel chevlai ... er ... (*Lost again.*

---

[21] *Yachny-divossy*: You gossip.

Tries again.) . . . Hamapeel chevlai shano, al anai . . . er . . . al anai . . . (*He gives up and continues in English.*) Blessed are Thou, O Lord Our God, King of the Universe. Please look after Mam and Dad and everyone, and let Hitler get a railing up his tochass.[22] Amen.

Scene 25
Ext. Waterproof-garment factory. Manchester. Morning.

> LOUIS *and* SARAH *walking briskly along the street, going to work. He wears a cloth cap, she a turban.*

SARAH (*V.O.*):   'Dear Neville and Danny . . . Just a line to let you know all is well at this end. Your dad's chest is better, he says, now that he's back on the Woodbines. He says at this rate he'll be after Frank Swift's job in the City goal. Joke.'

Scene 26
Int. Factory. Day.

> LOUIS *is at his bench, varnishing mackintosh sleeves to the body of the coat. At other benches, men of* LOUIS's *age are working. One of these is* BERNARD. SARAH *passes carrying a high pile of cut-out sleeves to another bench.*

SARAH (*V.O.*):   'We're both busy at work, where everyone says the war will definitely be over soon, as the Germans are without butter and starving.'

> *A* WOMAN *from the 'office' approaches, distributing pay-packets from a tray. She hands* LOUIS *his. He immediately looks at the details on the back.*

LOUIS: A pound??
WOMAN: A pound clear. You had a dead horse to work off from *last* week.
LOUIS: How the hell do we manage on a pound?
WOMAN: The manager says we'll be on government orders soon. Tons of work. Army coats, capes, everything. Be like the good old days.
BERNARD: When were *they*, sweetheart?

Scene 27
Ext. Street 'B', Cheetham Hill. Day.

> WILHELM *desultorily playing marbles, alone, where he watched the boys playing marbles earlier.* SARAH *approaches, carrying shopping-bag.*

---

[22] *tochass:* backside.

SARAH (*V.O.*):   'It's pretty quiet on the street these days, without you and the other boys fighting, and breaking windows. But we're getting used to it.' (*She smiles at* WILHELM.) Hello. (WILHELM *lowers his eyes.* SARAH *offers him a chocolate bar from her shopping-bag.*) Buzz Bar? (WILHELM *shakes his head and moves away.* SARAH *smiles and continues towards her house.*) (*V.O.*) 'And I had a nice long chat with that foreign boy today, Wilhelm, who sends you his regards.'

Scene 28
Ext. Street 'C', Cheetham Hill. Day.

SARAH *passes* MERTON *who's leaning against a wall, blowing up a football with a bicycle pump. She smiles at him. He watches her ankles as she walks on. He gives her a wolf whistle. She looks back quietly amused and walks on.*

SARAH (*V.O.*):   'Not forgetting Merton, the footballer, who's getting quite a big boy now.'

Scene 29
Int. The Millers' living-room. Night.

GRANDMA *is asleep in the chair, mouth hanging open, her prayer book still in her hand.* SARAH *sits at the table writing her letter. On the table, ready to be parcelled up, are a cooked chicken and other items she mentions.*

SARAH (*V.O.*):   'I'm enclosing a cooked chicken with helzel, and some marzipan cake, and two chocolate Buzz Bars. And a balaclava helmet each I've knitted. They're both the same, so no fighting.' (*The sirens start wailing.*) 'Your grandma is with me at the time of writing' (*she glances across at* GRANDMA *who's now snoring*) '. . . and sends her love. She was listening to Lord Haw-Haw[23] on the wireless yesterday – and said she knows who he really is. Guess who? Jack Buchanan[24] acting the goat! Anyway, that's all for now. I'll be over to see you soon, and be good boys to Mr and Mrs Graham. Lots of love, and keep warm. Pip, pip, pip. Your loving Mam and Dad.'

A.R.P.[25] WARDEN (*O.O.V.*)[26]:   Put that bloody light out!

SARAH *gets up, switches the light off, and by the light of the fire, pops the letter into a cardboard box – into which she starts parcelling the food.*

---

[23] *Lord Haw-Haw*: the nickname given to William Joyce, the English traitor who made propaganda broadcasts from Germany during the war.
[24] *Jack Buchanan*: a popular musical comedy star of the time.
[25] *A.R.P.*: Air Raid Precautions.
[26] *O.O.V*: out of vision.

Scene 30
Int. Mrs Graham's kitchen. Morning.

> *On the table is the parcel* SARAH *sent – now opened.* MRS GRAHAM *is reading* SARAH's *letter. She then stuffs it into her apron pocket and exits towards the lounge.*

Scene 31
Int. Mrs Graham's lounge. Continuous in time.

> DANNY *and* NEVILLE *are reluctantly polishing the furniture.*

DANNY: We'll be late for school!
NEVILLE: Tell us one we don't know, clever!

They continue polishing for a moment.

DANNY: We're always late!
NEVILLE: Shurrup – or we'll have more to do tonight.

> MRS GRAHAM *enters from the kitchen.* DANNY *and* NEVILLE *at once start polishing furiously.*

MRS GRAHAM: Boys – there's been a letter from your mother.

They stop work and look up at her expectantly.

MRS GRAHAM: Everyone's very well at home, and she hopes you're both being good boys. (*She smiles at them good-humouredly.*) And you are, aren't you? Specially when you're asleep! Do you get it?
NEVILLE: Please can we read it – the letter?
DANNY (*finishing* NEVILLE's *sentence for him*):   Mrs Graham?
MRS GRAHAM: Oh, I didn't think. I've thrown it away now. But she's sent you a nice parcel.
DANNY (*hopeful excitement*):   Stuff to eat??
MRS GRAHAM: Two lovely balaclavas to keep your ears cosy. So she hasn't forgotten you, has she? (*The boys swallow their disappointment.*) Have you written to *her* this week? (DANNY *looks at* NEVILLE *for guidance.* NEVILLE *stares ahead, lips sealed.*) Remember your mother said you'd to be good.

Another tiny hesitation, then DANNY *takes a letter from his pocket, before* NEVILLE *can stop him.*

DANNY: We just need an envelope.
MRS GRAHAM: I'll get one for you. And post it.

> *She grabs the letter from him, and starts scanning through its pages, as she exits to the kitchen.* DANNY *frustratedly realizes he's been conned. His eyes look as though they're about to fill up again.* NEVILLE *swiftly belts him one.*

Scene 32

Ext. Blackpool promenade. Afternoon.

A small squad of R.A.F. recruits are being drilled by their instructor. NEVILLE, DANNY *and* ZUCKERMAN, *each carrying his satchel, pass by – showing no interest in the R.A.F. men (they've seen similar sights many times before).* DANNY *is running his Dinky Toy racing car along the rail. As he walks:*

ZUCKERMAN: Why don't you kill her?
NEVILLE: How?
ZUCKERMAN: Sabotage. Shoot her with a tommy-gun.
NEVILLE: You're barmy, you!

There's a pause. DANNY *and* NEVILLE *are very morose.* ZUCKERMAN *is trying to decide whether to confess a secret. He finally decides he will.*

ZUCKERMAN (*quietly*):   I'm going to escape.

DANNY *and* NEVILLE *look at him, puzzled but impressed. They stop walking.*

ZUCKERMAN: I'm going home. Back to Manchester.
DANNY: When?
ZUCKERMAN: Soon.
NEVILLE: How?
ZUCKERMAN: I've got a secret plan.
DANNY: What is it?
ZUCKERMAN: I haven't just worked it out yet.

They stand silently, preoccupied. DANNY *looks at* NEVILLE *to see if the thought of escape interests him.* NEVILLE *starts off towards home.* ZUCKERMAN *starts off the other way.* DANNY *starts following* NEVILLE.

ZUCKERMAN (*turning*):   Do you want to come in on it?
DANNY (*promptly*):   Yes!!
NEVILLE (*reluctantly*):   No.
DANNY: Go on, our kid!
NEVILLE: I said no!

ZUCKERMAN *walks on.*

DANNY (*muttering behind* NEVILLE):   We might. You never know. It's only irrelevant.

They walk on.

Scene 33

Ext. Sand dunes 'A', South Shore. A little later on.

DANNY, *with great interest, and* NEVILLE, *against his will, are surreptitiously trailing a teenage girl across the dunes.*

NEVILLE: You don't know what 'irrelevant' even means.
DANNY: I do!
NEVILLE: What, then?
DANNY (*evasively*):   Just 'cos *you* don't . . .

The girl descends into a hollow between the dunes. DANNY *and* NEVILLE *creep to the brow of the dune and peer over. The girl runs to a young soldier who's sitting there waiting for her. They go into a clinch.* DANNY *and* NEVILLE *turn away disappointed.*

NEVILLE: I told you she wasn't a spy.

They walk on.

Scene 34
Ext. Sand dunes 'B', South Shore. A little later.

DANNY *and* NEVILLE *are still walking home. We suddenly hear a piercing sound, like the mating-call of a bird whose voice is breaking.* NEVILLE *stops dead in his tracks. Other calls — many other calls — come from different directions, replying to the first.* NEVILLE *takes* DANNY's *arm. They stand looking round. From their P.O.V.[27] we pan round the grassy tops of the dunes which surround them, in a full circle.* DANNY *and* NEVILLE *are now both very alarmed. Suddenly, from behind each dune, a small boy steps forward. They all begin to converge on* DANNY *and* NEVILLE *in a circle. They stop a yard or so away and their* RINGLEADER *steps forward.*

RINGLEADER: Where are *you* going then?
NEVILLE: Nowhere.
RINGLEADER: It's *our* say who goes across here. What gang are you in?
NEVILLE: We're not in any.
RINGLEADER (*suspiciously*):   You're not from round here, are you?
NEVILLE: Manchester. (*Pronounced 'Manchister'.*)
RINGLEADER: Where??
DANNY: Manchester. (*Pronounced 'Manchister'.*)

The RINGLEADER *turns to his gang, laughing.*

RINGLEADER: They can't even *say* it right! (*To* DANNY *and* NEVILLE) It's Manchester, not Manchister! (*His gang laughs.*) Isn't it?
DANNY: Yes. (*Pronounced 'Yis'.*)

The RINGLEADER *again roars with laughter. His gang join in.*

---

[27] P.O.V.: point of view.

RINGLEADER: Do you want us to let you go?
DANNY: Yes. (*Pronounced 'Yis'.*)

The gang roars with laughter.

RINGLEADER: Say it again!
NEVILLE: No.
RINGLEADER: I said, say it again!
NEVILLE: No.

The RINGLEADER *gives his bird-call as a signal and the whole gang immediately attack* DANNY *and* NEVILLE. *A violent mêlée of arms, legs, punches – punctuated throughout with piercing bird-call war-cries.*

Scene 35

Int. Mrs Graham's lounge. Teatime.

MR *and* MRS GRAHAM *are seated at the table, ready to begin their meal.* DANNY *and* NEVILLE – *with the odd cut, bruise and sticking plaster on their faces, are standing at the table, in their normal places for eating, except that, this time, nothing has been laid out for them.*

MR GRAHAM (*head lowered*):   For what we're about to receive, may the Lord make us truly thankful. (DANNY *and* NEVILLE *look at their empty plates.*) Amen.
MRS GRAHAM: Amen. (*She and* MR GRAHAM *begin eating. The boys just stand there.*) Little boys who won't learn that fighting is wrong get no tea. (*The* GRAHAMS *continue eating.*)
DANNY: Not even a pork sausage, Mrs Graham?
MRS GRAHAM: Were you given permission to speak?
DANNY (*thinks for a moment*):   Oh, no.

They stand there in silence, apart from the clatter of MR *and* MRS GRAHAM's *knives and forks.*

Scene 36

Int. The boys' bedroom. Evening.

The same evening. DANNY, *wearing pyjamas and schoolcap, is standing by the wall, re-positioning small swastikas and Union Jacks on a wall-map of France.* NEVILLE *is in bed reading a comic. From downstairs we hear the muted sounds of 'ITMA' on the wireless (or 'South of the Border').*

DANNY: Why is it always *us* withdrawing and not the Germans?

NEVILLE *is preoccupied throughout the whole scene with his comic.*

NEVILLE: To fortify positions or summat.
DANNY: Is that good?
NEVILLE: Yes. (*Pronounced 'Yis'.*)
DANNY: It's 'Yes' not 'Yis'!
NEVILLE: No, it isn't.
DANNY: That's why they battered us!
NEVILLE: No, it wasn't.

DANNY *looks at him, puzzled.*

DANNY: I thought it *was* ...?
NEVILLE: It was because they're Nazis.
DANNY: Who?
NEVILLE: Them kids. Just because we're not in their gang.

DANNY *gets into bed and curls up, with his back to* NEVILLE. *Silence for a moment, apart from the wireless downstairs.*

DANNY: I'm going to tell my mam about Mrs Graham.

NEVILLE *looks up for the first time from his comic.*

NEVILLE: You're bloomin' well *not*, our kid!
DANNY: I am!
NEVILLE: I'll belt you! She's got enough to worry about. You tell her nothing, okay? Except we're dead happy. (DANNY *lies there, his eyes open, staring miserably into space.* NEVILLE *relents a little.*) Hey, our kid. Look.

He shows DANNY *a 1940 pin-up of a girl in a bathing costume which has been torn from a magazine – and which he'd been looking at the whole time, hidden between the pages of his comic.* DANNY *looks at it, unimpressed, not at all sure why he's been invited to look at it.*

DANNY: It's a lady in a bathing costume.
NEVILLE (*smirking*):   I know.
DANNY: What about her?
NEVILLE (*grinning*):   You know ...
DANNY: What?
NEVILLE (*giving up*):   Nothing. Go to sleep ...

They try to settle down to sleep, both very hungry.

DANNY: Neville? Say for instance someone had no tea. How long would it be before they died?
NEVILLE: Go to sleep.
DANNY: If they got no breakfast either, they might be skeletons by school-time.
NEVILLE: There's a war on. You have to tighten your belt.
DANNY: I can't. My pyjama elastic's broke.

We hear MRS GRAHAM *O.O.V., walking up the stairs.* NEVILLE *quickly yanks* DANNY's *cap off.*

NEVILLE: Hey up! She's coming!

DANNY *grabs his cap back and puts it on again. They both lie back feigning sleep. The footsteps get nearer. At the last possible moment,* DANNY *pulls his cap off and holds it under the bedclothes.* MRS GRAHAM *pops her head into the room, peers first at one then the other and, satisfied they're asleep, switches the light off and exits, to return downstairs.* DANNY *lies there in semi-darkness.*

DANNY (*to himself*):   Blessed art Thou, O Lord our God, King of the Universe. Look after Mam and Dad and everyone, and let Hitler get cut up into little pieces with bayonets, and then burnt alive in boiling oil, then thrown in quicksand up to his neck while the ants eat him. And let him die slowly with toothache and horrible gashes. (*Pause*) And the same goes for Mrs Graham. Only double.

Scene 37
Int. Mrs Graham's lounge. Continuous in time.

MRS GRAHAM *enters and starts tidying the room.* MR GRAHAM *is sitting reading the evening paper. The radio music audible in the previous scene continues.* MRS GRAHAM *picks up* DANNY's *jacket from behind a chair to hang it up, when suddenly she holds it to her face and strokes it tenderly against her cheek. Guiltily she glances at* MR GRAHAM *to see if he saw her. He did, but quickly looks away. She briskly folds the jacket and continues tidying up. She glances back at her husband but he's now reading again.*

Scene 38
Ext. Street 'C', Cheetham Hill.

A *queue of Jewish women are standing gossiping outside a grocery shop. The queue is hardly moving at all into the shop.* GRANDMA *approaches, sees the queue, and decides to join it. Caption: '19 May 1940'.* GRANDMA *stands behind the last woman in the queue and exchanges a smile of recognition with her.*

GRANDMA: So what are we queuing for?
WOMAN IN QUEUE: About three hours by the looks of it, believe me!
GRANDMA: Nu?[28] How's the family, please God?
WOMAN IN QUEUE (*an enigmatic shrug*):   Ah.
GRANDMA (*enigmatic nods of the head*):   Mmmm.

---

[28]*Nu?*: Well?

WOMAN IN QUEUE: Yours?

GRANDMA: The same. (*Pause*) And Yankel? He's enjoying jumping the parachutes?

WOMAN IN QUEUE (*proudly*): A lance-corporal now, conohorry![29]

GRANDMA: That's good.

WOMAN IN QUEUE: Like Works Manager.

GRANDMA (*pleased*): Mazeltov![30]

WOMAN IN QUEUE: And little Danny and Neville?

GRANDMA: Thank God. (*Meaning 'all right'.*)

WOMAN IN QUEUE: Thank God. (*Meaning 'thank God'.*)

GRANDMA: Today they have their mamma. Every month she's there like a calendar. (*Sighs*) Nine months now, already – who's counting...?

Scene 39
Ext. Blackpool pier. Day.

Open on an extremely pregnant girl sitting on a bench facing the sea. She's the girl from the sand dunes (in Scene 33). She's knitting baby clothes. Track back to see that she's the first of a long line of women – all seated on benches, all knitting and all very pregnant. SARAH, DANNY *and* NEVILLE (SARAH *hand-in-hand with each of them*) *are walking along from the prom towards the pregnant women.* DANNY *and* NEVILLE *are wearing their balaclavas, now well worn.* SARAH *is singing a favourite song of theirs, trying to jolly them up.* NEVILLE *joins in now and then where he remembers the words.* DANNY *isn't in the mood.*

SARAH/NEVILLE (*singing*):
> Cheese and bread,
> The old cow's head,
> Roasted in a lantern,
> A bit for you,
> And a bit for me,
> And a bit for Molly Dancers!
> Cross-a-Molly,
> Cross-a-Molly,
> Cross-a-Molly Dancers!

As they pass by the pregnant women, DANNY *stares at them, absolutely intrigued.*

DANNY: Is it a knitting contest?

SARAH: Ssssh. Don't stare. Not nice.

---

[29] *conohorry*: pronounced kane-ane-haw-reh; may no evil eye harm him.
[30] *Mazeltov!*: Congratulations!

DANNY: They've all got fat bellies.

NEVILLE: They're all pregnant.

DANNY: What's 'pregnant'?

SARAH (*staring at* NEVILLE):   Where did you hear that word?

NEVILLE: Sidney Zuckerman. It's not swearing. 'Nackers' is swearing.

SARAH (*shocked*):   Do you know what that *means*?

NEVILLE (*nonchalantly*):   It doesn't mean nothing. It's just swearing.

SARAH (*relaxing again*):   Oh, I see.

DANNY: What's 'pregnant'?

SARAH: They're having babies.

DANNY (*craning his head round to look at them*):   What – now?

SARAH: Soon. They've come here so's the babies won't get bombed.

> *They walk on.*

DANNY: I thought they might've been spies.

NEVILLE: He thinks *everyone's* spies.

SARAH (*stopping*):   Hey! you two! (*They stop and look at her. She takes a greaseproof-paper parcel from her shopping bag.*) Salt beef sandwich or Buzz Bar? (*The boys leap in delight.*)

DANNY: High-ho, Silver!

NEVILLE: Both!!

Scene 40

Ext. Blackpool pier. A little later.

> DANNY *and* NEVILLE *are munching away at their sandwiches.*

DANNY: Anyway – any German spy could stick a pillow up his jumper and sit there pretending he's pregnant.

NEVILLE: Shurrup, our kid. He gets on your nerves.

> SARAH *watches them a moment as they eat with enormous gusto.*

SARAH: And are you still happy with Mrs Graham?

NEVILLE (*promptly*):   Yes.

SARAH: No complaints?

NEVILLE:.   No.

SARAH: And you still don't get homesick?

NEVILLE: No.

SARAH: Danny?

NEVILLE (*before* DANNY *can open his mouth*):   He doesn't either.

Scene 41

Ext. Photographer's stall on the pier. An hour or so later.

SARAH, DANNY *and* NEVILLE *stand with only their faces visible poking through the cut-outs in a huge 'comic scene' canvas. All three are laughing and giggling. The* PHOTOGRAPHER *is preparing to take the picture.*

PHOTOGRAPHER (*good-humouredly*):   Now, settle down, you three! We haven't got all day.

DANNY *immediately becomes conscious of the time and stops laughing.* SARAH *realizes the reason for his sudden sadness.*

DANNY: What time is it?

SARAH *smiles at him, understandingly.*

SARAH: I don't go back for *hours* yet...
DANNY: No one said you do. It's irrelevant.

Scene 42
Int. The Millers' living-room. Evening.

GRANDMA *is in her chair dozing – mouth wide open. From the wireless comes the voice of* WINSTON CHURCHILL.

CHURCHILL (*V.O.*):   'I speak to you for the first time as Prime Minister in a solemn hour for the life of our country, of our Empire, of our Allies, and, above all, of the cause of Freedom...'

Scene 43
Ext. Street 'B', Cheetham Hill. A few minutes later.

LOUIS *is walking down the street towards his house. He carries a length of wood cut out into the shape of a rifle. The wireless of each house is tuned to Churchill, so that, as* LOUIS *passes the houses, we hear Churchill's speech continuing – its volume rising and falling with each house.*

CHURCHILL (*V.O.*):   '... Behind them – behind us – behind the armies and fleets of Britain and France – gather a group of shattered States and bludgeoned races...'

LOUIS *passes* WILHELM, *who is against his wall, playing with a yo-yo or whip and top.* LOUIS *winks at him.*

CHURCHILL (*V.O.*):   '... the Czechs, the Poles, the Norwegians, the Danes, the Dutch, the Belgians – upon all of whom the long night of barbarism will descend, unbroken even by a star of hope, unless we conquer, as conquer we must; as conquer we shall...'

LOUIS *turns into his own doorway.*

Scene 44

Int. The Millers' living-room. Continuous in time.

> GRANDMA *wakes up on hearing the front door bang.* LOUIS *enters. He's still carrying the rifle-shaped piece of wood. Churchill's speech continuous on the wireless.*

CHURCHILL (*V.O.*): '... Today is Trinity Sunday. Centuries ago words were written, to be a call and a spur to the faithful servants of Truth and Justice: Arm yourselves...'

> GRANDMA *sees the 'gun'* LOUIS *is holding and screams.*

CHURCHILL (*V.O.*): '... and be ye men of valour, and be in readiness for the conflict...!'

LOUIS: It's not real!

GRANDMA: Oy libbergott![31]

LOUIS: It's a piece of wood! That's all we get in the L.D.V.s.[32]

GRANDMA (*unconvinced*): I know! I know! Just don't point, it's rude. Anyway, it might go off.

CHURCHILL (*V.O.*): '... As the will of God is in Heaven, even so let it be.'

Scene 45

Int. Mrs Graham's lounge. Continuous in time.

> MRS GRAHAM *is helping* SARAH *into her coat.* SARAH*'s case and shopping-bag are at her feet – ready packed for her journey home.*

MRS GRAHAM: There we are, dear.

SARAH: Thank you.

> DANNY *and* NEVILLE *are sitting side by side on the settee watching their mother with sinking hearts.*

DANNY: Can we come to the station, Mam?

NEVILLE: To see you off, Mam?

MRS GRAHAM (*before* SARAH *can reply*): Oh, it's much too late for little boys to be out, isn't it, Mrs Miller, of course it is.

> SARAH *stands, ready but reluctant to go.*

SARAH: Well... I'll... I'll love you and leave you. Thanks for putting me up again, Mrs Graham.

MRS GRAHAM: Our pleasure, wasn't it, children? (SARAH *stands there – the boys watching her.*) It's a shame you can't stay a little longer, really...

SARAH: Yes. (*To the boys*) I'll be back next month. We'll have fun *again*.

MRS GRAHAM (*laughing indulgently*): Oh, they never stop, them two! My

---

[31] *Oy libbergott*: Oh, dear God.
[32] *L.D.V.s*: Local Defence Volunteers, the precursor of the Home Guard.

husband terms them Jewell and Warriss, after the comedians.

SARAH *smiles at the boys.*

SARAH: I'll say ta, ra, then.

DANNY *and* NEVILLE *stand up.* SARAH *glances at* MRS GRAHAM *to see if she intends to leave them in private to say their farewells.* MRS GRAHAM *stays firmly put, smiling politely.* SARAH *resigns herself to it. She kisses the two boys.*

SARAH: Danny. Neville.

DANNY: ⎫
NEVILLE: ⎭ Ta, ra, Mam.

SARAH: Be good boys now. See you very, very soon. Pip, pip, pip.

She picks up her shopping-bag and small case and exits with MRS GRAHAM *following her out. The two boys stand there.* DANNY *takes his Dinky Toy racing car from his pocket quietly, vrumm-vrumms it on the table for a moment, then puts it back in his pocket. We hear* MRS GRAHAM *and* SARAH *bidding each other goodbye at the door. The door bangs to.* MRS GRAHAM *re-enters and starts busying herself tidying up.*

MRS GRAHAM (*briskly, businesslike*): Isn't she nice? Lovely hair, hasn't she?
DANNY (*with quiet pride*): She dyes it. She's a peroxide blonde. I used to watch her doing the roots.

Scene 46

Ext. Blackpool street. Evening.

SARAH *walks down the street, away from the house. She's very close to tears.*

Scene 47

Int. Boys' bedroom. Later the same night.

DANNY *is re-positioning swastikas on his wall-map . . . The Union Jacks continuing their retreat towards Dunkirk.* NEVILLE, *in his pyjamas, is about to get into bed. He stops at the dressing-table and takes his comic from his satchel. He opens it and starts to take from it his pin-up, which is hidden between the pages. He changes his mind, puts the pin-up back into the comic, and the comic back into his satchel. He slings the satchel on to the floor and climbs into bed. From downstairs we can hear the wireless play the opening signature tune of 'The Happidrome'.* DANNY *gets into bed. For the first time, it's* NEVILLE *who quietly starts to cry.* DANNY *turns – and is about to start crying himself. Instead he bites his lip – and belts* NEVILLE *across the head.*

Scene 48

Ext. Bicycle shed, school playground. Day.

> *From inside a nearby classroom, we hear a class of boys chanting in unison 'Cargoes' by John Masefield.* ZUCKERMAN *appears, creeping surreptitiously from the back of the shed. Bundled in his arms are his cap, coat, haversack, gas-mask case and paper parcel. From the parcel he takes a pair of roller-skates and starts putting them on, keeping a wary look-out as he does so.*

Scene 49

Ext. Another part of school playground.

> NEVILLE's *class are playing football, dressed in their normal school clothes.* NEVILLE *is in goal. The 'goalposts' are bundles of jackets put down by the boys. While play is at the other end* NEVILLE *is standing on his own. He suddenly picks up one of the 'goalposts' – which is composed of his own cap, coat, haversack and gas-mask case – and dashes off with them, towards the bicycle shed.*

Scene 50

Ext. Boys' toilets, playground.

> DANNY *emerges surreptitiously from the toilets, carrying his clothes and haversack, etc. He walks along with an innocent nonchalance for a few yards, then suddenly makes a frantic dash towards the bicycle shed.*

Scene 51

Ext. Bicycle shed, school playground.

> ZUCKERMAN *is now fully dressed, his haversack on his back, and is fastening his roller-skates on.* NEVILLE *is beside him – also fully dressed. He takes a pair of roller-skates from his coat pockets and starts fastening one of them on.* DANNY *arrives, struggling hurriedly into his coat and haversack.* NEVILLE *passes him his other skate.* DANNY *starts putting it on. They speak conspiratorially.*

ZUCKERMAN: Did you ask to leave the room?
DANNY: Yes.
ZUCKERMAN (*alarmed*):   To wee? That's what *I* said!
DANNY: No, a bilious attack. (ZUCKERMAN *watches the others fastening on their single skates.*) Do you think you'll be okay with just one each?
NEVILLE: Prisoners of war don't even have *none* even!

They continue getting ready, with ZUCKERMAN *– just a little scared – keeping look-out.*

ZUCKERMAN: Ready?

NEVILLE: Hang on a sec!

ZUCKERMAN: Say 'Roger and Out' when you are.

DANNY: How will we know the way – with all the signposts blacked out?

ZUCKERMAN: I've got a compass.

NEVILLE: And a map?

ZUCKERMAN: I can't follow maps.

NEVILLE (*incredulously*):   Well, what good's a— You're barmy, aren't you! What are you?

ZUCKERMAN: We'll ask people the way. Not coppers, though. Or we'll be nackered. Ready?

DANNY: Yes.

NEVILLE: Yes.

ZUCKERMAN: Say 'Roger and Out'.

DANNY/NEVILLE: Roger and Out.

Stealthily they skate out of the school-yard and into the street – DANNY *and* NEVILLE *running on one foot and skating on the other.*

Scene 52

Ext. Blackpool, street 'D'.

The three of them are skating along. They pass a newsagent's placard: 'B.E.F. evacuates Dunkirk'.[33]

Scene 53

Ext. Blackpool, street 'E'.

The three of them are skating along.

Scene 54

Ext. Blackpool promenade.

ZUCKERMAN *and* NEVILLE *skating along.* ZUCKERMAN *is wearing his gas-mask.* DANNY *is falling further and further behind and appears to be in trouble. Suddenly his skate collapses. He stops.*

DANNY (*calling*):   Our kid!!

NEVILLE *and* ZUCKERMAN *stop and turn.*

---

[33] *B.E.F.*: British Expeditionary Force.

NEVILLE: Trust you! Orky Duck ...

NEVILLE and ZUCKERMAN *skate back to* DANNY, *who shows them his skate. Two of the wheels have broken off.*

DANNY: Are we nearly there?

ZUCKERMAN: We're not even in Preston yet.

A pause. Nobody knows what to do. ZUCKERMAN *takes off his gas-mask.*

ZUCKERMAN: Have you got the busfare back?

NEVILLE: I've got a shilling.

DANNY: You two go on ...

NEVILLE: No. Zuckie can. I'll come back with you.

DANNY: No, Nev! It's your big chance.

NEVILLE: No. She'd only put you in solitary confinement.

He starts taking his skate off. The others watch unhappily.

DANNY: Can we *walk* it to Manchester!!

NEVILLE (*shaking his head*):   Too far.

ZUCKERMAN (*sympathetically*):   Best go back, Danny.

DANNY *nods sadly. An uncomfortable silence.*

ZUCKERMAN: Ta, ra, men.

NEVILLE: See you after the duration, Zuckie.

ZUCKERMAN: If I collect any shrapnel, I'll save you some.

He hitches up his haversack, puts his gas-mask on again and skates off on his way. DANNY *and* NEVILLE, *fed up, frustrated, start off back to Blackpool.* NEVILLE *gives* DANNY *a dirty look – which* DANNY *notices.*

DANNY (*tearfully*):   It wasn't *my* fault!!

NEVILLE *launches into him, fists flying; they fight and wrestle for a few moments.* NEVILLE *gets* DANNY *to the ground and straddles over him, then suddenly stops – struck by a sudden thought.* DANNY *looks up from his vanquished position.*

DANNY: Do you give in?

NEVILLE (*half to himself*):   He could've given you one of his!!

DANNY: What?

NEVILLE (*getting up*):   We could've had one skate each! (*He shouts down the road.*) Zuckie! Zuckie! Wait!

In vain ... ZUCKERMAN *is out of sight.* NEVILLE *shrugs.*

NEVILLE (*sighing*):   Come on. Deadly Nightshade.

He starts tramping off back towards Blackpool. DANNY *gets up and trudges after him.*

Scene 55

Int. The Millers' cellar. Night.

> *The furniture is composed of boxes and blankets. To one side is an area piled high with coal.* SARAH *is knitting. The sounds of an air-raid are not too distant.* GRANDMA *enters, wearing a pinny and carrying a saucepan of soup and a soup-ladle.*

GRANDMA: Who wants some nice chicken soup, yes? Ask a meshugganah[34] question – everybody!

> SARAH *mutters* 'No, thanks'. GRANDMA *waits a moment, then tries again.*

GRANDMA (*temptingly*):   Warms the kichkes,[35] nice . . . (*She smacks her lips. Again,* SARAH *declines her offer.*) Nice drop of chicken soup for the air-raid. Special recommended. (*Again,* SARAH *refuses.*) Do you good when the bombs drop. The King and Queen have it.
SARAH: How can chicken soup do you good if you're blown to smithereens?
GRANDMA: God forbid! (*She spits three times.*)
SARAH: Wouldn't do you any good *then*, would it?
GRANDMA (*shrugs*):   It wouldn't do you any *harm* . . .

> GRANDMA *turns to exit back upstairs, as* LOUIS *enters, putting on his cap and coat and carrying a torch.*

GRANDMA (*to* LOUIS):   A meshugganah missus you've got. (*She exits.*)
LOUIS: See you later.
SARAH: I thought Bernard was fire-watching tonight?
LOUIS: So, I'll *help* him, terrible thing! Ta, ra.

> *She calls* 'Ta ra' *after him as he exits. The sounds of the air-raid become nearer and heavier.* GRANDMA *re-enters, carrying a saucepan.*

SARAH: You won't take no for an answer, will you!
GRANDMA (*sitting on a box*):   It's a different pan, what you talk? This one's milkadicky.[36] (*She inverts it and puts it on her head as a helmet.* SARAH *laughs.*) Nu? Someone told you a good joke? Issy Bonn,[37] maybe? Laugh – gezuntereit!

Scene 56

Ext. Factory. Night.

> *Smoking debris and rubble. The scream and exploding roar of bombs. Shouts, whistles, burning wood. Perhaps an ambulance and fire engine.*

---

[34] *meshugganah*: crazy.
[35] *kichkes*: innards, guts.
[36] *milkadicky*: made of milk.
[37] *Issy Bonn*: a Jewish comedian.

Scene 57
Int. Factory. Night.

> *Smoke, debris. Outside, bombs are falling and buildings burning.* LOUIS, *together with* BERNARD (*another fire-watching employee*) *and a* FIREMAN, *is standing over a corpse, which is half covered by a blanket.* LOUIS *and* BERNARD *are coming to the end of 'Yitgadal' – the Hebrew prayer of mourning. They're wearing their caps; the* FIREMAN *holds his helmet in his hands. A* ST JOHN AMBULANCE MAN *clambers in, sees the corpse.*

AMBULANCE MAN: He's the only one, is he?
FIREMAN: Incendiary in the yard. He came rushing in . . . Got half the roof on his head . . .

> *The* AMBULANCE MAN *bends over the body. The corpse is* MERTON – *the budding footballer from Scene 5.*

AMBULANCE MAN: Bit of a kid . . .
FIREMAN: Used to run messages for us on his bike . . . Marvellous footballer, I believe.
AMBULANCE MAN (*getting up*):   Not any more . . .
FIREMAN: No. Seventeen. Breaks your heart.
LOUIS: Fifteen.
FIREMAN (*puzzled*):   You have to be seventeen before you can . . .
LOUIS: Honest. He was a pal of my two lads. I'd best go and tell his mam.

Scene 58
Ext. Blackpool Station.

> DANNY *and* NEVILLE *standing waiting to meet* SARAH *off the train. The train pulls in. Passengers – mostly service men and women – get out.* DANNY *and* NEVILLE *look, with growing anxiety, up and down the quickly emptying platform. A* SAILOR *gets out.*

NEVILLE: Mister!
SAILOR: The Navy don't have cap-badges. Ask a soldier.
NEVILLE: No . . . just is this train from Manchester?
SAILOR: Yes.
DANNY: Are you sure?
NEVILLE: Thank you.

> *The* SAILOR *walks off.* DANNY *calls after him.*

DANNY: Are you positive?

> *The* SAILOR *ignores him.* DANNY *and* NEVILLE *stand peering disconsolately down the platform. No one else gets off. They're left alone.*

NEVILLE: Come on.

DANNY: Why hasn't she come?

NEVILLE: Stop shlurrying[38] your feet.

He prods DANNY *towards the barrier. As they go, sadly, we hear* SARAH, *voice over.*

SARAH (*V.O.*):   'Dear Neville and Danny, Just a quick line to let you know all is well at this end. I'm sorry I couldn't come on Saturday as promised, only your Dad's been off work a few days owing to an accidental fire at the factory. Someone must have dropped a cigarette-end or something. So to get some extra pennies and get the war over quicker, I've stayed to do some overtime. I hope you didn't mind, and I'll definitely be over before you can say Jack Robinson. Everyone sends their regards. All your pals and everyone is very well, so there's nothing to worry about, is there? Be good boys to Mr and Mrs Graham. Lots of Love. Pip, pip, pip. Your loving Mam and Dad.'

(**Scenes 59 to 64** are a montage sequence. Musical link – early war pop-song.)

Scene 59

Ext. Grocery shop, street 'C', Cheetham Hill.

The broken shop-window is boarded up with planks across which is a painted: 'Business as usual'. GRANDMA *walks into the shop, carrying her purse and shopping-basket.*

Scene 60

Int. Grocery shop.

The shopkeeper, MR GROSSFINE, *is giving* GRANDMA *one egg.*

GRANDMA: So what's this, Mr Grossfine?

MR GROSSFINE: This week's ration, Mrs Miller.

GRANDMA: Very nice. Monday I'll bake with it. Tuesday I'll chop herrings with it. Wednesday I'll fry it. Thursday I'll boil it. Friday, with a bit of mazel,[39] I'll sit on it, and hatch chickens of my own...

MR GROSSFINE (*shrugs*):   Mrs Miller. Is it my fault?

GRANDMA (*firmly*):   Mr Grossfine, I want a dozen. (*Ingratiatingly*) I knew your father, ovoshalom.[40] With no tochass in his hazen.[41]

MR GROSSFINE (*wearily*):   Pass me your ration book. I'll explain.

---

[38] *shlurrying*: dragging, shuffling.
[39] *mazel*: good luck.
[40] *ovoshalom*: may peace be with him.
[41] *with no tochass in his hazen*: when he had no seat to his trousers.

GRANDMA *hands him her identity card from her shopping bag.*

MR GROSSFINE: That's your identity card. I want your ration book.

GRANDMA: Blackshirt!⁴² (*She raps his knuckles.*) Nah!

Scene 61
Int. Munitions factory.

SARAH *is working with two or three more women at a bench. They wear goggles and use welding equipment. They're singing an early war pop-song in accompaniment with a vocalist on the wireless. A* MAN IN OVERALLS *passes, carrying a crate labelled 'W/D⁴³ bullets 837/9'.*

MAN IN OVERALLS: Here you are, Sarah. For your Louis.

He takes a cigarette-lighter, made in the shape of a bullet, from the crate, flicks it alight to test it, and gives it to her.

SARAH: I thought we were making *bullets*?

MAN IN OVERALLS: Ssshh. Careless talk costs lives.⁴⁴ Have another. (*He hands her another lighter.*)

Scene 62
Ext. Synagogue, Cheetham Hill.

From inside, we hear the chanting of Hebrew prayers. One of the windows is broken. Over it is a piece of cardboard on which is painted: 'Business as usual'.

Scene 63
Int. Synagogue.

Two men, wearing yarmulka or hat, and tallis (long shawl), are chanting Hebrew devoutly from their prayer-books. (More voices off, chanting in unison.) Still chanting, the first man takes from his raincoat pocket a bag of Tate & Lyle sugar and hands it, without looking, to the second man. He, in turn, takes from his pocket a paper bag. The first man takes it, opens it to reveal a piece of raw steak, nods, closes it again. Both men pocket their exchanged goods, and devoutly continue praying.

---

⁴² *Blackshirt!*: Fascist!
⁴³ *W/D*: War Department.
⁴⁴ *Careless talk costs lives*: a war-time slogan.

Scene 64
Ext. Street 'B', Cheetham Hill.

A woman is rushing down the street, knocking on each door, then opening each door and calling inside – 'Mrs Levi! Bananas at the Co-op!' 'Mrs Abrams! Bananas at the Co-op!' 'Mrs Miller . . .' SARAH *emerges from her front door, struggling into her coat.*

SARAH: I heard! I heard!

She, MRS LEVI *and* MRS ABRAMS *dash out of their houses and race off down the street towards the Co-op. The woman continues knocking at each door and calling the good news.*

Scene 65
Int. Mrs Graham's lounge. Evening.

Open on DANNY *and* NEVILLE *eating bananas. They're sitting round the fire with* MRS GRAHAM *and* SARAH *– who is on the latest of her visits. In evidence are one or two games – Ludo, Snakes and Ladders, etc. It's late Sunday afternoon – an hour or so before* SARAH *is due to catch her train home again. Consequently,* DANNY *and* NEVILLE *are in fairly subdued moods.*

SARAH: Another game, kids?
DANNY: You haven't time. Your train goes in—
SARAH: How about 'I Spy'?
MRS GRAHAM: I think they're probably a little overtired . . .
SARAH (*thinking of a game*): I know! 'Silly Story'!
NEVILLE: What's that?
SARAH: You get a piece of paper and everyone writes down a—
DANNY: I can't play it.
MRS GRAHAM: You don't know what it is yet, child!

She smooths his hair down maternally. SARAH *notices – but pretends that she hasn't.*

SARAH (*to the boys*): I write the beginning of a story – something silly – and fold the paper over so's the next one can't read it. Then he writes *his* daft sentence, and folds it over and passes it to the next and—
DANNY: It's silly.
NEVILLE: That's the idea, barm-pot.
SARAH: And when we've all finished, we read the whole thing out, and it makes a Silly Story – and we all laugh!
MRS GRAHAM (*to the boys*): I'll show you.

MRS GRAHAM *takes pencil and paper and starts writing, laughing to herself at her story.* DANNY *sits watching solemnly and ignores* SARAH's *reassuring smile.* MRS GRAHAM *folds the paper and passes it to* NEVILLE, *who starts writing.*

DANNY: I won't know what to put...

SARAH: Whatever comes into your head.

An idea is slowly forming in DANNY's *mind. He seems scared – and a little excited...* NEVILLE, *grinning at what he's written, folds the paper and hands it to* DANNY. DANNY *looks at each of them tensely.*

MRS GRAHAM: You put whatever you *want*, child! (DANNY *reaches his decision. He starts writing thoughtfully. The others watch him – amused at his concentration.*) Come on, slowcoach!

DANNY *continues writing, tongue stuck out in concentration.*

NEVILLE (*impatiently*): Oh, blimey!

DANNY *finally folds the paper and hands it to* SARAH. *She starts writing, smiling at her story.* DANNY *sits nervously looking from one to the other.*

DANNY: Read it.

SARAH: In a minute. (*She finishes writing and unfolds the paper.*) Right. (*Reading*) 'Once upon a time, there were two princes called Danny and Neville who lived in a Castle called Blackpool Tower, with the other monkeys!'

SARAH *smiles at* MRS GRAHAM, *who smiles back, proud of her story.* SARAH *unfolds the paper further and continues with* NEVILLE's *contribution.*

SARAH (*reading*): '... And then the Spitfires attacked the Messerschmitt, and the German pilot shouted "Get off my foot!"'

She, NEVILLE *and* MRS GRAHAM *laugh.* DANNY *watches the paper in* SARAH's *hands, tensely.* SARAH *unfolds it again and starts to read* DANNY's *contribution.*

SARAH (*reading*): 'She is dead cruel to us. She steals your letters and ... (SARAH *stops and looks at* DANNY. *He sits impassively.* MRS GRAHAM *stares from one to the other, blankly.* SARAH *slowly resumes reading, aloud...*) 'She is dead cruel to us. She steals your letters ... and whatever you send us. She makes us clean and polish the house every day, and gives us rotten dinners. She hates us. And we hate her back. All this is secret. We want to come home.'

She lowers the paper on to her lap. Everyone seems frozen to stone – except SARAH.

SARAH (*quietly, calmly*): Is this true, Danny?

DANNY (*quietly*): Yes, Mam.

SARAH: Emess?

DANNY: Emess adashem.[45]

SARAH (*turning to* NEVILLE):   Neville?

NEVILLE (*nodding, scared*):   Yes, Mam.

SARAH *turns to* MRS GRAHAM.

SARAH: Mrs Graham?

Scene 66

Int. The Millers' living-room. Evening.

It's the first night of 'Chanuka' – the Jewish Festival of the Lights. The eight-stemmed candelabrum is in the centre of the table. LOUIS *is seated at the table, wearing his yarmulka, sorting out the prayer-books, ready to start the informal family service.* DANNY, NEVILLE *and* SARAH, *led by* GRAND-MA, *who holds aloft a lighted candle, are doing a wild conga round the room. They're singing, as follows.*

ALL: 'Mo outsur y'shuosee / L'cho noeh / L'shabeyach / Teecoun base t'filosee / V'shom toudoh / N'zabeyach ... Mo outsur y'shuosee[46] – (*Then even more loudly*) The cat's in the cupboard and he can't see me!!!

LOUIS: Yes, all right. Can we get started now?

GRANDMA *lights the first candle with the one she's holding, then places it into the centre holder.*

LOUIS (*to the boys*):   Now, you know why we're doing this, don't you?

DANNY: 'Cos we haven't got a shilling for the meter!

NEVILLE (*parrot-fashion*):   The festival of Chanuka is to commemorate the return of the Israelites to the Temple, after forty years in the wilderness. In the Temple there was—

DANNY: Dad asked *me*!!

NEVILLE (*ignoring him*):   ... there was only enough oil in the lamp to last for one day, but—

DANNY: Mam, stop him!

NEVILLE: ... But God worked a miracle—

DANNY: Anybody knows that!

NEVILLE: ... and it burned for eight days instead.

DANNY (*hastily to* LOUIS):   So we light a candle each night for eight nights, till they're all lit! Amen. (*He pulls his tongue at* NEVILLE.) Clever-dick!

The sirens begin to sound. They all fall silent. SARAH *looks at the clock.*

SARAH: Ten minutes early tonight.

---

[45] *Emess adashem*: Honest to God.

[46] *Mo outsur y'shuosee ... y'shuosee*: 'O Fortress, Rock of my salvation...', the opening of a hymn chanted every night for eight nights during the Chanuka festival.

Scene 67

Int. The boys' bedroom (Blackpool). Evening.

> *The room looks sparse and bare. All the boys' belongings have gone –
> including* DANNY's *wall-map. There's a sudden, heavy silence in contrast to
> the noise of the previous scene.* MRS GRAHAM, *her eyes empty, is stripping the
> beds down to their mattresses.* MR GRAHAM, *evening paper in his hand,
> appears at the door. He smiles briefly, stiffly, at her, in an awkward
> attempt at cheeriness.*

MRS GRAHAM (*quietly, evenly*):   He tells lies, young Danny, I *didn't* hate them.

MR GRAHAM: 'Course not...

MRS GRAHAM: I taught them respect, yes. Agreed. To respect their elders and
betters. I wouldn't say that was cruel.

MR GRAHAM: Only way really...

MRS GRAHAM: I'd say that was love. That's the word I'd give it. (*Pause*) Her
love isn't love at all. Too *much* love...

> *A pause*

MR GRAHAM: Not to worry ...

MRS GRAHAM: No. (*She works silently for a moment.*) *That's* what's cruel.
(*She looks at him.*) I asked her to let me adopt them ... officially...

MR GRAHAM: Come downstairs, love ...

MRS GRAHAM (*fighting the tears*):   I had to make them try and forget her,
Gordon, hadn't I?

> *He looks at her uneasily.*

MR GRAHAM: Their own *mother*?

MRS GRAHAM: *I* was their mother!

> *A silence. They stand looking helplessly at each other.*

MR GRAHAM (*going to her*):   Come on, love.

> *She allows herself to be led to the door, his arm round her shoulder.*

MR GRAHAM: Attagirl ...

> *They exit.*

Scene 68

Int. The Millers' cellar. Night.

> *Aircraft flying in waves overhead. Bombs screaming nearby.* DANNY,
> NEVILLE, SARAH *and* GRANDMA *are now all sitting with saucepans on their
> heads – and all a little nerve-racked.*

NEVILLE (*addressing the German bombers*):   Hurry up, I'm tired. I want to gay schloffen.[47]

DANNY (*abruptly*):   Don't you start, German sausage!

NEVILLE (*puzzled*):   What?

DANNY: Spouting German! It's bad enough with *her*! (*Meaning* GRANDMA.)

SARAH (*shocked*):   Danny!

NEVILLE (*defensively*):   It wasn't German. It was Yiddish.[48]

DANNY: It's the same thing!

NEVILLE: It never is – is it, Mam?

GRANDMA (*puzzled*):   All the Yiddishe talk Yiddish – that's why they're Yiddishe...

DANNY: It's German!

GRANDMA (*shouting*):   So it's German. Does that make it *German*?

DANNY (*almost crying in anger*):   It's the Germans who are bombing us!

They sit there quietly. Disturbed. The All Clear begins to sound. They start gathering their things to return upstairs.

GRANDMA: All of a sudden he's anti-Semitic against the Jews...

NEVILLE *bursts into laughter.* GRANDMA *looks at him puzzled.*

GRANDMA: Nu?

NEVILLE: You can't be anti-Semitic against the Christians, can you!

DANNY, *angrily silent ever since his outburst, exits upstairs.* NEVILLE *watches him go.*

NEVILLE: What's got into the little rabbi?

SARAH: He's growing. I can tell by his clothes.

Scene 69

Int. The Millers' living-room.

A little later the same night. DANNY, *in pyjamas, is re-lighting the principal candle in the candelabrum. He starts then lighting the remaining eight – which are not too firmly stuck in their holders.*

Scene 70

Int. Parents' bedroom. Continuous in time.

SARAH *is in bed.* LOUIS *is undressing for bed.*

---

[47] *gay schloffen*: go to sleep.
[48] Yiddish: language used by Jews in or from central and eastern Europe. Many words in Yiddish come from German.

LOUIS: Town was hit bad, I believe. Blackfriars ... Cannon Street. And Trafford Park got another pasting. The docks...
SARAH (*calling*):   Danny, are you in bed yet?
DANNY (*O.O.V.*):   Nearly.
SARAH (*calling*): What are you doing down there?

Scene 71

Int. The Millers' living-room. Continuous in time.

DANNY *is gazing expressionlessly at the row of burning candles.*

DANNY (*calling*):   Nowt. (*He exits.*)

Scene 72

Int. Parents' bedroom. A few minutes later.

SARAH *and* LOUIS *are lying in bed.*

LOUIS (*slightly troubled*):   Danny said a rum thing. When I told him about Merton being dead. I said his mam and dad were heartbroken ... their only son being killed. He said, 'So what? They can always have another.'

Scene 73

Int. The boys' bedroom. Continuous in time.

DANNY *and* NEVILLE *are lying in their beds.*

NEVILLE: Goodnight, our kid.
DANNY: Goodnight.

NEVILLE *settles down to sleep, then suddenly starts up again.*

NEVILLE: Hey! Can you smell burning?
DANNY: No?

We hear the crackling of wood burning downstairs. The bedroom slowly fills with smoke.

DANNY: Yes!!

The boys leap out of bed.

NEVILLE: Dad!! (*He races to the door.*) Dad, the house is on fire!

We hear doors banging, running feet, shouting. DANNY *is sitting on the edge of his bed, struggling to get his socks on.*

DANNY (*calling out*):   It must be a time-bomb. Delayed action.
LOUIS (*O.O.V.*):   Downstairs – all of you – quick!

SARAH (*O.O.V.*):   Danny, come on! Mother – never mind your teeth!

DANNY (*calling*):   It could be a Molotov Bread-Basket.[49] With delayed action.

SARAH *dashes in, in dressing-gown.*

SARAH: Not the only one, is it? (*She drags him out, with one sock on.*)

Scene 74

Int. The Millers' living-room. Continuous in time.

LOUIS *is stamping on what's left of the curtains, which are in flames on the floor. There are smouldering burns on adjacent furniture, the ceiling and carpet. The tablecloth is burnt to ashes.* SARAH, GRANDMA, NEVILLE *and* DANNY *are huddled together in the doorway watching* LOUIS *put out the fire. We hear A.R.P. whistles outside, and men's voices shouting.*

DANNY: Was it a Molotov Bread-Basket, Dad?

LOUIS *sighs, picks up the blackened candelabrum and looks at him pointedly.*

LOUIS: No, Danny. A bloody candle!

We hear more A.R.P. whistles and, much to DANNY'S *horror, a fire engine approaching with bells ringing. The family all turn to look at* DANNY *accusingly.*

DANNY (*faintly*):   Oy, gevalt...[50]

Scene 75

Int. Classroom. Day.

The room is empty apart from ZUCKERMAN *and* DANNY. *It's some months later.* DANNY *now wears* NEVILLE'S *old cast-offs, and* ZUCKERMAN *wears spectacles. They're taking out* MR GOLDSTONE'S *desk drawers and putting them back upside down.* DANNY *is rummaging in his satchel. He gets out his Dinky Toy racing car, and places it beside a lump of shrapnel on his desk. He looks from one to the other, trying to evaluate their worth.*

DANNY: Will you take this for it? (*He holds up the racing car.*)

ZUCKERMAN: What – for a real piece of landmine?

DANNY: Are you sure it's not just ack-ack shell?

ZUCKERMAN: Any money.

---

[49] *Molotov Bread-Basket*: a cluster bomb, which broke up in flight to scatter a large number of small incendiary bombs. Molotov was Soviet Minister of Foreign Affairs during the Second World War.

[50] *Oy, gevalt*: Oh, help!

The door opens and MR GOLDSTONE *enters with a ten-year-old boy, who's wearing cap, coat, gas-mask case round his shoulders, identification label, and carries a suitcase.*

MR GOLDSTONE: You two know the bell's gone?

DANNY:
ZUCKERMAN: } Yes, Sir.

MR GOLDSTONE: Got no homes to go to?

DANNY:
ZUCKERMAN: } Yes, Sir.

DANNY: Please, Sir, I'm just waiting for my brother from Standard Five.

ZUCKERMAN: Please, Sir, I was helping the ink-monitor.

MR GOLDSTONE: Either of you live near Elizabeth Street?

DANNY:
ZUCKERMAN: } Yes, Sir.

MR GOLDSTONE: Good. (*He takes some papers from his desk and gives them to the small boy.*) Take this boy to Mrs Bloom, Number 110, Elizabeth Street. She's taking him in. He's an evacuee from London. Philip Hyman. Philip's just arrived. Say hello to each other.

DANNY:
ZUCKERMAN: } Hello.

PHILIP: Hello.

MR GOLDSTONE: See you in the morning, Hyman.

PHILIP: Yes, Sir.

MR GOLDSTONE *exits.*

DANNY: I used to be an evacuee when I was a kid.

PHILIP: So what?

He stands watching DANNY *put his racing car back in his satchel and rummage for something else to swap.* PHILIP *notices the bathing-beauty pin-up photo which* NEVILLE *had in Blackpool sticking out of the satchel; he takes it and looks at it – now very dog-eared and creased.*

PHILIP: Who's this?

DANNY: No one! (*He grabs it back from* PHILIP *and stuffs it back into his satchel.*)

Scene 76

Ext. Street 'D', Cheetham Hill. Half an hour later.

DANNY, NEVILLE, ZUCKERMAN *and* PHILIP, *carrying his suitcase, are walking towards Elizabeth Street. One or two other boys from school are some little distance behind them, walking home. A little further behind is* WILHELM, *walking home alone.*

NEVILLE (*to* PHILIP):   What do you reckon to Manchester, then?

PHILIP (*very strong Cockney accent*):   'S all right. Can't grumble.

DANNY *stops dead in his tracks and stares at him with amused incredulity.*

DANNY (*mimicking*):   'Grumble'?? 'Grumble'?? Got a right Cockney twang, hasn't he?

NEVILLE: Shurrup, our kid. (*To* PHILIP) We get air-raids here an' all, you know...

PHILIP: Not like us. We get *tons*. Every night.

DANNY *is now hysterically beside himself at* PHILIP's *accent.*

DANNY (*mimicking*):   'Tons'!! Every 'night'! (NEVILLE *and* ZUCKERMAN *find it difficult not to laugh. To* PHILIP) It's 'tons' and 'night' (*both with Manchester pronunciation*), not 'tons' and 'night' (*Cockney pronunciation*).

PHILIP: No, it ain't.

DANNY: Say it again. Say 'grumble'.

PHILIP: I shan't.

DANNY: I said, say it again!

PHILIP: I heard you!

DANNY *pins him against a wall. On it is chalked 'Open the second front now!'*[51]

DANNY: Say it again!

PHILIP: Bugger off!

DANNY *promptly laces into him and punches him in the stomach.* PHILIP *groans.*

PHILIP: You rotten pig! I've just had my appendix out!

DANNY (*dropping his fists, then, sympathetically*):   Sorry.

PHILIP *promptly punches* DANNY *in his unguarded mouth.*

NEVILLE: Look, quit it, you two!

DANNY (*inarticulately*):   He's knocked a tooth loose!

NEVILLE (*grabbing his arm*):   Come on. (*He starts leading* DANNY *away.*)

DANNY (*inarticulately*):   Rotten Londoner... (*He points to his teeth.*) Look. That one.

NEVILLE (*pushing him*):   Get home.

WILHELM *has now drawn level with them.*

NEVILLE (*to* WILHELM, *not expecting a reply*):   Hi-de-hi.

WILHELM (*grinning*):   Ho-de-ho!

---

[51] *Open the second front now*: a call to invade German-occupied France and so help the Russians.

NEVILLE (*amazed*):   Hey, Danny! Hear that! He *spoke*! Wilhelm *spoke*!!

DANNY *tries to tell* WILHELM *about his loose tooth – but the words are an incoherent mumble. He pulls his jaw open, to show the damage.* WILHELM *smiles at him – and walks on alongside* NEVILLE, ZUCKERMAN *and* PHILIP. *They all talk among themselves.* DANNY *trundles behind, holding his jaw, mumbling to himself. They walk on towards Elizabeth Street ... away from camera.*

SUGGESTIONS FOR WRITING AND DISCUSSION

1 *From what you learn in this play, describe what it is like for a child to be evacuated and what his or her family feel.*
2 *From what you learn in this play, describe what life was like for civilians during war.*
3 *What do you learn about Jewish life from this play?*
4 *Describe the kind of family life the Millers had.*
5 *Describe how the author manages to convey to the viewer/reader the setting of his play and the period of time in which it takes place.*
6 *Describe the Grahams and their attitudes and feelings towards Neville and Danny.*
7 *Describe Grandma and her importance in the play.*
8 *Describe two scenes which you found moving and explain why.*
9 *Describe two scenes which you found comic and explain why.*
10 *In a television play the writer can make his effects with great economy, using very few words. Illustrate this with reference to a number of scenes.*
11 *Outline the importance of some of the minor characters (for example, Merton, Zuckerman, Wilhelm) to the effect of the play.*
12 *Do you think the writer convincingly conveys the feelings and behaviour of junior school children? Justify your answer with examples.*
13 *Comment on the differences in character between Danny and Neville, and the feelings they have for each other.*
14 *Pick out the incidents in the play which indicate conflicts based on 'being different' (for instance, race, religion, accents) and comment on them.*
15 *Do the characters in this play and the situations they are in arouse your sympathy? Justify your answer with examples from the play.*
16 *What would you say are the main differences between reading this play and seeing it on television?*
17 *If you were writing a review of this play, on what factors would you say its appeal and success are based?*
18 *Write a story or a play about being evacuated.*
19 *Write a story or a play about living in a city during a war.*

20 *Choose one of the minor characters in the play and develop a story or play around him or her.*

21 *What do you think it would be like to be an evacuee? If it happened to you what would you worry about and how would you behave?*

22 *Write a brief account of any group of people at the present time who are evacuees or refugees. Give as much background as possible; you could write about Palestinian or Ugandan or Ethiopian refugees.*

23 *As a group, collect a dossier of people's different recollections (and mementoes) of the Second World War. This will mean inquiring from neighbours and friends, and perhaps your own family, about their experiences. You could include recorded interviews and spoken recollections as well.*

24 *Choose either the Grahams' house, or the Millers', and give detailed instructions for the set.*

25 *Find out what you can about how factories – such as the one where Louis and Sarah work – were converted during the war from, for instance, clothing to munition factories. What work was involved in these factories during the war? Was any training necessary? Were women employed in the manufacture of munitions? Prepare a display on war work in factories and give a talk on it. Each member of the group could take a different aspect, for example: retraining; how women were affected; what was produced and how it was packaged; factory regulations for reasons of secrecy and security; wages, and so on.*

26 *Write a script for a television play about a child whose foster parents want to adopt him or her, but the child's natural parents will not agree.*

27 *Write about a time when you have been with other people and have felt very different, or out of place – because they spoke a different language, or because you had a different accent, came from a different background, and so on.*

28 *Write about a family visitor who comes to stay for a while and who speaks with an accent or in a dialect of English which you all find hard to follow. You could write it as a play or a short story, or you could improvise it.*

NADINE GORDIMER

Nadine Gordimer was born near Johannesburg, South Africa, in 1923. She began writing at the age of nine and published her first story at fifteen. She still lives in South Africa, although she also travels widely, lecturing on modern African literature. Her collections of short stories include *Not for Publication*, *Friday's Footprint*, *Six Feet of the Country*, *The Soft Voice of the Serpent* and *A Soldier's Embrace*. Among her novels are *The Late Bourgeois World*, *A Guest of Honour*, *The Conservationist*, *Burger's Daughter* and *July's People*. Her writing has won many awards and international recognition.

As with most of her writing, *A Chip of Glass Ruby* deals with relationships between men and women and with the effects of living under an oppressive regime. It is one of a series of screenplays based by the author

on her own short stories in *Six Feet of the Country*, and it is interesting to compare the screenplays with the stories and to see how the stories have been at the same time expanded and simplified. The short story of *A Chip of Glass Ruby* begins with the arrival of the duplicating machine. The Special Branch policemen arrive and take Mrs Bamjee away. The story ends with Girlie wishing Mr Bamjee a happy birthday. In the story, there are nine children, Mrs Bamjee being a widow with five children of her own before she married Mr Bamjee.

It is also interesting that Nadine Gordimer calls her treatment a screenplay rather than a television play, and in some ways the treatment is more like that of a film than a television play. This approach is becoming more prevalent in television today.

The play has been banned in South Africa and has not been shown there.

A CHIP OF GLASS RUBY

CHARACTERS

MR YUSUF BAMJEE	1ST NEIGHBOUR
MRS ZANIP BAMJEE	2ND NEIGHBOUR
JIMMY	AFRICAN COUNTRYWOMAN
GIRLIE	AFRICAN ICE-CREAM VENDOR
AMINA	YOUNG INDIAN WOMAN
AHMED — THEIR CHILDREN	WHITE CUSTOMER
FAROUK	INDIAN IN TRAIN
FARIDA	INDIAN FLOWER-SELLER
MRS HASSIM	TWO WARDRESSES
MRS HASSIM'S FATHER	MOSES
DR ABDUL KHAN	MOHAMMED
MRS NDAWO	WHITE CHILD
MR MASHISHI	ORIENTAL PLAZA SHOPKEEPER
SCOTTISH WOMAN	TWO AFRICANS IN TAXI
AFRIKAANS WOMAN	TWO AFRICAN WOMEN
AFRICAN MAID	INDIAN AND COLOURED
AFRICAN COOK	HIGH-SCHOOL CHILDREN
WHITE POLICEMAN	TWO COLOURED POLICEMEN
ELDERLY INDIAN	

To help the actors and director, Nadine Gordimer supplied the following notes on the characters in *A Chip of Glass Ruby*.

MR BAMJEE is in his early sixties, a worn, morose, taciturn man who has received little or no formal education. He and his family are Muslims. He is probably a descendant of indentured labourers who came (principally) from Gujerat, India, throughout the second half of the nineteenth century (beginning in 1860) to work on the sugar plantations in Natal, South Africa. His mental horizon is bounded by the daily round of his produce lorry; he is self-employed, barely literate, and preoccupied with retaining, even as a poor man in a humble position, the niche he has been thrust into in the hierarchy of the colour bar. He can always feel himself *at least* better than a black man (African) since, although the law discriminates against him in many ways, he does not carry a pass. He is thick-set, very dark, and moves heavily.

MRS BAMJEE is in her mid/late forties, gentle, affectionate, with a natural high intelligence that compensates for lack of education. She was perhaps once good-looking; she is faded with child-bearing and hard work, but still exerts a strange attraction, quite unselfconsciously and without a will to power, over everyone in her orbit. Her strong sense of justice is as natural to her as her love for her family; her compassion is a revolutionary force in itself. She is thin and long ago ceased to have any vanity, or time for care of her personal appearance, although she observes the decent conventions of Muslim dress for women. Quintessentially feminine, she is the type that comes to be claimed by feminists as a heroine, in spite of herself.

GIRLIE is the BAMJEES' eldest child. She is about twenty, married to MOHAMMED, and expecting her first child. She is a typical contemporary Johannesburg Indian girl from a lower-middle-class family. She dresses in cheap fashionable European clothes, has cut her hair and wears make-up, chews gum and talks in the breezy, kidding fashion favoured by city youngsters of all colours.

JIMMY is sixteen/seventeen. He has inherited his mother's fineness and intelligence. Being young, he does not express himself as naturally as she does, but uses current platitudes, dogmatism, that nevertheless do not detract from the sincerity of his political commitment.

AMINA, a beauty, fourteen/fifteen, has inherited her mother's gentle and devoted nature, but without the underlying strength. There is the sense that something of her childhood is being lost under the strain put upon her by her position as her mother's helper and substitute.

AHMED is about ten, intelligent and lively.

FAROUK is eight, equally intelligent and lively.

FARIDA, the baby of the family, is five/six.

DR ABDUL KHAN is a successful doctor from a family with a long tradition of political activity, dating from his grandfather's association with the early passive resistance against unjust laws, initiated by the South African Indian Congress in association with Mahatma Gandhi himself. DR KHAN is economically and socially superior to the BAMJEE family, but he and MRS BAMJEE belong in a fraternity of social and political awareness that crosses all boundaries.

MR MASHISHI is an efficient, worldly African academic administrator who, since the students' movement reactivated Africans politically, has set aside personal ambition 'within the (white) system' and joined the adult back-up movement.

MRS NDAWO is a middle-aged African, almost the conventional black Mamma in dress and appearance, as one would expect from her background as a churchwoman and worker on black self-help projects of the domestic kind. But in spirit she has now more in common with the Amazonian female in Delacroix's painting *La Liberté guidant le peuple* in the Paris of 1830 . . .

Scene 1
Ext. City. Day.

> *A hawker's lorry rocking down a city street. It bears the legend:* Y. E. BAMJEE LICENSED HAWKER FRESH FRUITS AND VEGETABLES DAILY. MOSES *clings nonchalantly to the tailgate.*

Scene 2
Photograph.

> *Titles over: faded photograph of Indian girl with red jewel in her nose.*

Scene 3
Ext. City. Day.

> *C.U.[1] of jewel dissolves to red carnations. Camera pulls back to reveal bunch of red carnations being lifted from tin of water at* INDIAN FLOWER-SELLER's *pavement stand, near Johannesburg City Hall, and being wrapped in a sheet of newspaper. Bunch of red carnations disappearing, carried away along busy street by* WHITE PURCHASER.

Scene 4
Ext. City/diagonal street Day.

> BAMJEE's *lorry rocking down a city street with his assistant,* MOSES, *hanging on the tailgate.*
> *End of titles.*

Scene 5
Int. BAMJEE *kitchen. Fordsburg. Day.*

> MRS ZANIP BAMJEE *pounding chillies. On kitchen table, typewritten draft of a document, which she reads as she works.*

C.U. text: 'DRAFT MEMORANDUM ON THE SITUATION OF BLACK TENANTS IN CENTRE CITY AREAS OF JOHANNESBURG.
Prepared by ACSTOP (Action Committee to Stop Evictions).
Shock statistics on the housing position for Indians and coloureds in the Johannesburg area have revealed that the Department of Community Development provided homes for only 947 Indian families last year out of a waiting list of 5,812. Of these, 1,533 have been waiting longer than five

---

[1] *C.U.*: close-up.

years for a home. The statistics were released only a day after the Minister of Community Development disclosed that the Administration Board had built no family housing units in Soweto last year . . .'

MRS BAMJEE *puts down the pestle, takes up a ball-point pen and makes a note or underlines something on the text.* FAROUK *beside her with a toy car.*

FAROUK: Farida's bust it!

MRS BAMJEE *smiles soothingly and replaces the wheel that has come off the car.*

Scene 6
Int. CMT factory. Day.

> GIRLIE *at work in a CMT (Cut, Make and Trim) clothing factory. She is highly pregnant; hums happily to herself.*

Scene 7
Int. BAMJEE *kitchen. Day.*

> MRS BAMJEE *turns page of memorandum.*

C.U. text: '. . . the housing crisis for African, Indian and coloured people arises from a policy which denies people available housing purely on an inhumane basis of skin colour . . .'

Scene 8
Int. BAMJEE *kitchen. Day.*

> MRS BAMJEE *pauses, in her double preoccupation of pounding chillies and reading text, to tie loose ribbon dangling from* FARIDA's *plait.*

Scene 9
Ext. Madressa school. Day.

> JIMMY *and* AHMED *coming out of Madressa (Muslim religious school attended after hours of secular schooling).*

Scene 10
Ext. White suburbs/city. Day.

> BAMJEE's *lorry.* BAMJEE *in the driver's cab.*

Scene 11
Int. BAMJEE *living-room. Day.*

    The living-room is shabby, poorly furnished, but rich in the evidence of human interests and activities centred there. The principal furniture crowded into a small space is a solid wood table, probably handed down, stiff-backed chairs to match, a sideboard, and a single, sagging armchair. Beside the armchair there is a fancy pedestal ashtray, never moved – that marks BAMJEE'S *territory. The sideboard is covered with a painted velveteen runner, and bears two vases of plastic flowers, a model of the Taj Mahal and a wedding photograph of* GIRLIE *and* MOHAMMED. *There is a large mantel clock. On the walls, an elaborate calendar, a mass-produced coloured portrait of Mahatma Gandhi, framed school certificates that witness to* JIMMY'S *prowess, a couple of class photographs from the other children's schools, a flowery cheap print of an idealized Indian landscape from the country no* BAMJEE *has ever seen. Newspapers and newspaper cuttings are piled up wherever there is space. A small glass-fronted cabinet holds books and family souvenirs – small ornaments, texts, etc., of the uplifting kind. There are children's comic-books and toys lying about. Yet the overall impression is of comfort, order and warmth.*

    MRS BAMJEE *at the table, studying spread of ACSTOP and black school boycott cuttings and papers. Camera holds on draft of SRC (Students' Representative Council) leaflet, handwritten, with many changes, etc.*

Scene 12
Ext. BAMJEE *house and Fordsburg Street. Day.*

    AHMED, FAROUK *and* FARIDA *burst out of* BAMJEE *house, go running through the streets of Fordsburg into Pageview Street. They pass* AMINA *among her girlfriends. She calls out some bossy warning. They run on; past removal notices, graffiti, empty shops, bulldozed areas, etc.*

Scene 13
Ext. Fordsburg Street. Dawn.

    Deserted street, BAMJEE'S *house; closed, burglar-proofed façade.*

Scene 14
Int. BAMJEE *bedroom. Dawn.*

    Alarm clock ringing. Face shows 4.45 a.m. BAMJEE'S *hand slams off alarm. Groans to himself softly beside sleeping* MRS BAMJEE.

Scene 15

Int. BAMJEE *kitchen. Dawn.*

Dressed, unshaven, BAMJEE *drinks tea in the kitchen. He wears shabby trousers of an old striped business suit, grubby shirt, hawker's white coat, and an old grey muffler round his neck.*

Scene 16

Ext. BAMJEE *yard. Dawn.*

BAMJEE *starting up his reluctant old lorry.*

Scene 17

Ext. Diagonal street/market. Early morning.

BAMJEE *at market/wholesaler, loading produce.* MOSES, *his African assistant (wearing jazzy track shoes, snappy denim dungarees, old woollen knitted cap pulled over his eyes), is half asleep, young and bleary. He grumbles in an African language to himself.*

BAMJEE: Put those onions at the back – not there . . . Come on! I don't pay you to sleep!

Scene 18

Ext. White suburb. Day.

BAMJEE's *lorry stationary in white suburban street. Picking over the produce are several customers from nearby houses: an elderly white woman who speaks with a Scottish accent, a middle-aged white woman with an Afrikaans accent, a pert African girl in smart maid's uniform, carrying a white toddler, an old African cook wearing a stained apron.*

SCOTTISH WOMAN: I want a branch of celery with my soup greens. Whatever'll I do with just those few carrots and leeks!

BAMJEE: No soup celery today. Only table celery, sixty cents.

SCOTTISH WOMAN: You keep your greens, then.

BAMJEE (*breaks stalk off table celery and tosses it in with the other greens*):   All right! I give you! But I myself I pay forty-five cents market-price!

AFRICAN MAID (*presenting her basket*):   For Mrs Williams. On the book. Three lemons, garlic, and give me nice tomatoes.

BAMJEE *weighs tomatoes. In grubby exercise book, notes money owed. Meanwhile,* AFRICAN MAID *takes apple from display and crunches into it, chatting with* MOSES *in an African language.*

BAMJEE (*indicating apple*):   Ten cents for that.

AFRICAN MAID (*jauntily*): Put it on the book. She must pay. Come, Snooks. (*Picks up child.*)

AFRICAN COOK: My madam want big lettuce. Why always you bring this small thing?

AFRIKAANS WOMAN (*pinching every avocado in box*): They no good. Everyone squeezes them, they all bruised . . .

BAMJEE: Only thirty cents each! The best!

AFRIKAANS WOMAN (*to* SCOTTISH WOMAN): Ag no, it's no use to buy from them . . . these days I rather go to the supermarket . . .

Scene 19
Ext. Pageview Street. Day.

Camera pans demolished houses. The roofs have been removed, doors and windows wrenched out. The inside walls, painted different colours, are testimony to people's individual home-making instincts; home is not just a roof over one's head. Among the demolished houses, a few still stand and are obviously occupied.

Scene 20
Int. Pageview House. Day.

Seen through window of small, semi-detached house, MRS BAMJEE *and another Indian woman,* MRS HASSIM, *sit at a table which almost fills the room. The room is a marked contrast to the hardly less modest living-room at the* BAMJEE *house. Here the walls are bare; no pictures, ornaments. No newspapers, papers, books. A cheap 'contemporary'-style sofa unit obviously doubles as a bed at night. A silent, white-bearded* OLD MAN *in the traditional tight-buttoned Muslim tunic and old sheepskin slippers, sits mute on the sofa. A 'dainty' tea with flowered paper napkins, cups for three, an iced cake and plate of* samoosas[2] *is laid at one end of the table.* MRS HASSIM *is taking dog-eared correspondence from a scuffed brown envelope.*

Cut to MRS BAMJEE, *a cup of tea steaming beside spread documents and her notebook.*

MRS BAMJEE (*refusing offer of second helping*): Thank you, no – that was delicious.

MRS HASSIM (*hovering*): Won't you try some cake?

MRS BAMJEE (*making notes*): Thank you, perhaps later.

Document in MRS BAMJEE's *hand:*

---

[2] *samoosas*: an Indian delicacy, small triangular pies filled with spiced mixed vegetables, then fried.

'REPUBLIC OF SOUTH AFRICA. DEPARTMENT OF COMMUNITY DEVELOPMENT. NOTICE TO TERMINATE OCCUPATION IN GROUP AREA.'

MRS BAMJEE: So you had this served on you – when – two years ago?

MRS HASSIM: The year my late mother passed away. Such a terrible time, I hardly took notice, you know . . .

C.U. document:

'WHEREAS the area defined was declared an area for occupation by members of the WHITE group . . . AND WHEREAS you are not a member of the WHITE group and therefore a disqualified person . . .'

MRS BAMJEE: I see they gave you three months to get out. What happened when you were still here last year?

MRS HASSIM: Well, we were very worried, but they didn't come . . . nothing . . .

MRS BAMJEE: You didn't apply for a house in Lenasia? You've never applied?

The OLD MAN *in his chair. He seems to exist on another plane; appears to hear or see nothing.*

MRS HASSIM: All that long way from town . . . My father – he was still – you know, quite himself, then. He didn't want to move. He is forty-three years in this house. I was born here. He said, let them carry me out . . . But now since we saw them pulling down the houses of people same like us . . . So we apply for a house and, after a long time, last week the Community Development send me a list of houses in Lenasia you can buy . . . But we haven't got money to buy a house. We tenants here forty-three years. I don't know what we going to do (*turns towards the* OLD MAN) if we can't find somewhere . . .

MRS BAMJEE: I'll copy these papers and return them . . . don't worry, we'll look after your father, we'll find something.

OLD MAN'S *face, slowly registering awareness of her presence.*

MRS BAMJEE (*V.O.*):   D'you think your husband would let us take you up as a test-case, in court?

The OLD MAN: *dignified, hostile, a frail monument.*

Scene 21

Ext. City street. Outside factory. Afternoon.

GIRLIE *coming out of factory after work. She meets her mother,* MRS BAMJEE. *They walk together chatting.*

GIRLIE: The girls at work did a test today, Ma.

MRS BAMJEE: A test?

GIRLIE: You hang your wedding ring by a piece of cotton over your stomach, if the ring turns one way, it's going to be a boy, the other way, it's a girl.

MRS BAMJEE (*tenderly amused*):   You believe that?

GIRLIE: Just a bit of fun...

MRS BAMJEE: What was the answer?

Scene 22

Ext. Mosque and Gandhi Building. Afternoon.

They approach the mosque, with an old tin mosque beside it.

GIRLIE: A boy. I hope it will be, anyway. Us girls were just saying at lunch-time... the men have the best of it. Even these days, we have to observe all the customs ... and we're not even allowed in there (*indicates mosque entrance*) with them...

MRS BAMJEE *is distracted by the sight of the old tin mosque, a ruin.*

MRS BAMJEE: Oh, look at that! It's going to collapse! It must be a long time since I walked along here...

GIRLIE: Someone used to store bananas there, when I was at school. Filthy old shack – why don't they pull it down?

MRS BAMJEE (*stops, takes her daughter's hand*):   Don't you know what it is? Seventy-six years ago, when Gandhi was living in South Africa, he planned the first mass protests against colour bar in that tin building. You will tell your little one, one day, you still saw it standing. Oh, if I had money...

Scene 23

Ext. Oriental plaza. Afternoon.

MRS BAMJEE *and* GIRLIE *buying baby clothes from stall in courtyard.*

GIRLIE: I'll just take the Babygrows (*measuring baby sleeping suits one against the other*) ... what d'you think, two first size and two second?

MRS BAMJEE: Oh, first size. Take the yellow, then it's right for boy or girl ... When the baby's bigger I want to make all the clothes...

GIRLIE (*indulgent*):   Ma ...! As if you've got time for that as well...

MRS BAMJEE: Of course I'll have time for that...

GIRLIE: Let's have a cool drink while I wait for Mohammed to come off work.

MRS BAMJEE: Thanks, but I think I must go now ... (*Pause; looks apologetically at her daughter.*) I must be at the house ... something is going to be delivered...

GIRLIE (*guessing, joking*):   Bajie's[3] hired a TV set!

MRS BAMJEE: Either this afternoon or this evening ... somebody's coming ... I must be there.

---

[3] *Bajie*: Daddy.

GIRLIE (*shields her mother from the eyes of the shopkeeper: looks at her closely and speaks very low*):   Oh, Ma ... (*long pause*) ... be careful...

Scene 24
Ext. Soweto Road. Dusk.

L.S.[4] *View of distant, endless stretch of uniform Soweto houses beyond road along which 2nd-class taxi (licensed to carry blacks only) is travelling. As the taxi draws level with, passes camera, it is seen there is a trunk/large laundry basket, roped up, between* TWO AFRICAN MEN *on the back seat.*

Scene 25
Int. BAMJEE *living-room. Evening.*

BAMJEE *family at supper.*

Scene 26
Ext. Fordsburg Street. Evening.

Arrival of 2nd-class taxi outside BAMJEE *house. The trunk/basket being carried from taxi by the* TWO AFRICAN MEN.

Scene 27
Int. BAMJEE *living-room. Evening.*

A duplicating machine being unpacked from the trunk/basket by MRS BAMJEE *with help of* JIMMY. AMINA *quickly clears away the supper dishes.* AHMED, FAROUK *and* FARIDA *look on interestedly and expectantly.* BAMJEE *has stopped in the middle of his task of rolling himself a cigarette (tin of tobacco, papers – everything for a fetishist ritual is laid out beside his pedestal ashtray and battered old armchair on a coffee stool). He looks at the machine as at some hostile invader settled in the house and, what is more, welcomed by his wife and family.* JIMMY *and* MRS BAMJEE *heave the machine on to the dining-table, the younger children smooth the rucked-up tablecloth.*

They have a sense of self-importance and enjoyment in being involved in a new element in the household. MRS BAMJEE *and* JIMMY *communicate in easy workmanlike phrases while the action takes place:* 'Careful, now, mind your fingers' (MRS BAMJEE) 'Just a sec—' (JIMMY) 'That's it', 'Move away, Farida', *etc.*

---

[4] L.S.: long shot.

AHMED (*sniffs at the machine like a little cat*):   It smells nice, just like Mohammed.

FAROUK (*face screwed up in exaggerated derision*):   Like *Mohammed*?

Everybody except BAMJEE *laughs at* AHMED.

AMINA: He's mad, man ... How can your sister's husband smell like a machine...?

MRS BAMJEE: No ... he means Mohammed's overalls ... the smell of grease, when he comes home from work at the garage...

AHMED: You *see*? Who says I'm mad...?

They laugh again. JIMMY *is opening reams of paper, tinkering to discover how the machine works.*

BAMJEE: A fine thing to have on the table where we eat.

MRS BAMJEE (*removing from sideboard two vases of plastic flowers,* GIRLIE's *wedding photograph, a plastic model of the Taj Mahal and the hand-painted velveteen runner*):   It's going to go nicely on the sideboard!

Scene 28

Int. BAMJEE *living-room. Same evening.*

Cut to: The pedestal ashtray beside BAMJEE's *chair, full of cigarette butts.*

Cut to: MRS BAMJEE *printing leaflets, standing at duplicator settled on the sideboard.* AMINA *doing her homework at the table.* JIMMY *ostensibly studying a schoolbook where he lies on the old sofa, but watching his mother.* AHMED *and* FAROUK *on their stomachs on the floor, grubby exercise books, atlas, etc., coloured pencils spread around.* FAROUK *drawing a huge, elaborate car.* AHMED *reading a violent comic-book. They are wearing pyjamas, like* FARIDA, *who plays some private game among the chair-legs. She has an old chocolate-box filled with buttons, broken necklaces, old Divali[5] cards, etc.*

BAMJEE *in his armchair. Doggedly he rolls himself another cigarette.* BAMJEE, *cigarette in his mouth, gets up and begins to walk out. He pauses to pick up one of the leaflets from the growing pile on the table. Text of leaflet, calling for boycott of African school classes, visible in his hand. He tosses down leaflet, hitting it with a gesture of the back of the hand.*

BAMJEE: Isn't it enough you've got the Indians' troubles on your back?

MRS BAMJEE (*turns obediently and gives him her respectful attention*):   What's the difference, Yusuf? We've all got the same troubles.

---

[5] *Divali*: Hindu festival of lights held in late October.

BAMJEE: Don't tell me that. We don't have to carry passes; let the blacks make trouble about their schools on their own. There are millions of them. Let them go ahead with it.

JIMMY: We're also black.

BAMJEE (*walking out*):   Of course, you are fifteen and you know everything. I have to earn the living, that's what I know. I'm the one who gets up four o'clock in the morning...

MRS BAMJEE (*smiling apologetically at* BAMJEE):   Not many more to do now...

> MRS BAMJEE *looks with solicitous concern at* BAMJEE's *weary back as he shuffles off to the bedroom.*
>
> *Cut to:* FARIDA, *asleep on the floor beside her box of rubbish.* AMINA *picks it up, starts rummaging.*

AMINA: Ma, look what I've found.

> *C.U. the flash of a red stone. Her fingers hold a small piece of cheap jewellery.*

AMINA: Pity, there's only one.

> *She holds it up against her ear-lobe, in which she wears a tiny gilt loop.*

MRS BAMJEE (*looking at her indulgently, reminiscently*):   Where did you find that?

AMINA: Farida was playing with this old box.

MRS BAMJEE: That's not an ear-ring, Amina. It's a nose ornament.

AMINA (*wrinkling her nose*):   A nose-ornament? From the olden days? Who wore it – your mother?

MRS BAMJEE (*feeding machine*):   It was mine. Let's see.

> AMINA *hands it to her mother.* MRS BAMJEE *looks at it.*

MRS BAMJEE: Yes ... I wore it. I haven't seen it ... years and years...

JIMMY: You wore a thing like that in your nose! I don't remember.

MRS BAMJEE: Oh, long before you were born ... before I was married ... As a young girl.

JIMMY (*disgusted*):   I can't believe it.

AMINA (*feminine, excited at the idea of her mother's youth*):   Put it on. How do you put it on?

MRS BAMJEE (*protesting, laughing*):   I can't. Not any more.

AMINA: Oh, come on, Ma, it's pretty. Why not?

MRS BAMJEE (*embarrassed, laughing, shy; she tentatively fingers the flange of her nostril*):   There was a hole – here – like you have in your ears. It's closed up, years ago.

AMINA: Oh, no ... I want to see you wear it ... It's precious, almost like a diamond – a ruby-stone, Ma—

MRS BAMJEE (*turning back to machine*):   I could never have a real ruby! It's only a chip of red glass.

AMINA (*fiercely*):   I don't care. If you wore it, it would look like a real ruby.
MRS BAMJEE: Too old-style, even for me.

Dissolve to MRS BAMJEE *alone, printing same leaflets. Every now and then she screws up her eyes with weariness then stretches them wide again to wake herself up. The mantel clock shows midnight. She sits, exhausted, in* BAMJEE's *chair. She fingers the place on her nose where once the glass ruby was. Dozes off.*

Scene 29
Photograph.

Dissolve to glimpse of photograph of INDIAN GIRL *with red jewel in her nostril.*

Scene 30
Ext. White suburban street. Day.

Cut to BAMJEE *weighing potatoes on a sheet of newspaper on his scale; he reads headlines about black schools boycott, student demonstrations.*

Scene 31
Int. BAMJEE *living-room. Day.*

MRS BAMJEE, DR KHAN, MRS NDAWO, MR MASHISHI *round living-room table. The pamphlets stacked ready in fruit and vegetable boxes obviously filched from* BAMJEE *stock.*

DR KHAN: ... out of the question! No students coming here to your place. It's simply leading the police to the door ...
MR MASHISHI: No, no, nobody must come here. Nobody must even know where the stuff is being printed.
MRS NDAWO (*stirs in agreement and makes African murmurs of assent*):   Yes, you must not be put in danger. You and our machine.
MR MASHISHI: I've got it all in hand – distribution points in different houses, Deep Soweto, Dube, Bosmont – I've liaised for tonight.
MRS BAMJEE: You don't have to worry about Indian schools – I've kept back enough for them.
MR MASHISHI: But *you* mustn't distribute – eh—
MRS BAMJEE: My son – he's got his team – I can trust him to do it all right.
DR KHAN: What about transport?
MR MASHISHI: Bob Mokhene's taxi again...?
DR KHAN: I don't think so. Better not. I'll get Vallabhai's dry-cleaner van. He'll do it.
MRS NDAWO: We should co-opt him on to the parents' committee.

DR KHAN (*smiling privately*): ... But he will help ... behind. He'll be ashamed to refuse me...

MRS NDAWO: Now, what about *our* leaflet? The Parents' Committee one we discussed at the last meeting? The young people expect to hear from us.

MR MASHISHI: It's done ... (*takes sheet of paper from his briefcase*).

MRS NDAWO (*looking up from reading sheet*): I think it should go out the same time as the students' one. If we want them to go on talking to us ... We must keep credibility.

She hands sheet to MRS BAMJEE.

MR MASHISHI: Tomorrow ...? How can we do that?

DR KHAN (*pauses, looks to* MRS BAMJEE): Depends what Mrs Bamjee can manage...

MRS NDAWO: It should be *right* away – right away...

MRS BAMJEE: I can do it tonight. How many copies? I don't know if there's enough paper – could you get some more?

Scene 32
Ext. BAMJEE's *street. Day.*

BAMJEE *drives his lorry past* DR KHAN's *large, new-model, well-polished car. He glances at it with dour recognition.*

Scene 33
Ext. BAMJEE's *yard. Day.*

BAMJEE *enters the yard, on foot, as* DR KHAN *is coming out.* BAMJEE *looks at* DR KHAN.

DR KHAN (*nods, a brief greeting, and speaks as he passes* BAMJEE): A wonderful woman.

Scene 34
Ext. BAMJEE's *street. Day.*

DR KHAN *getting into his car.*

Scene 35
Int. BAMJEE *kitchen. Same day.*

MRS BAMJEE *preparing ingredients for supper. Around her,* AMINA, FARIDA, FAROUK. FAROUK *playing;* FARIDA *tugging at her mother's trousers, and displaying a tear in her dress;* AMINA *idling, filching a taste of this and that.*

MRS BAMJEE: It's really a shame if you're tired of lentils, Farouk, because that's what you're getting – Amina, hurry up, get a pot of water going.

FARIDA *begins to whine and pull at the tear in her dress.*

MRS BAMJEE: Don't worry, I'll mend that in a minute. Be a good girl and just bring the yellow cotton; there's a needle and everything in the cigarette box on the sideboard.

FARIDA *whines and stamps her foot.*

MRS BAMJEE: All right, Mommy will fetch it.

Scene 36

Int. BAMJEE *living-room. Same day.*

Cut to: JIMMY *reading newspaper in the living-room.* MRS BAMJEE *looking for needle and cotton.* BAMJEE *enters.*

BAMJEE: Was that Dr Abdul Khan leaving?

MRS BAMJEE *turns as if it were only a mannerism that makes* BAMJEE *appear uninterested in politics. She persistently interprets his hostility as an endearing gruffness hiding boundless goodwill.*

MRS BAMJEE: Yes. We had the meeting here instead of at Mangera's place because he's gone to have a tooth out. And the leaflets are ready, anyway...

BAMJEE: What for do you want to get mixed up with these burnings and stonings and I don't know what? Isn't it enough with the Group Areas? Isn't it enough we can be thrown out of here? Any day we can be told to pack up and go. Put out in the street. I haven't got money to buy a house like Dr Abdul Khan in Lenasia. Who will make a noise and throw stones at the police when you and your children are without a roof? Are your black friends going to give you a place to live?

MRS BAMJEE (*softly, slowly*):   Yusuf... A white government tried to send your own grandfather back to India, although this was the country of his birth, same as theirs... You told me that many times. When they started moving Indians in other towns, you said we should only begin to worry when we get moved out of our own houses here... Nobody's safe. What happens to Soweto children happens to our children. What they do to people in Soweto one year they will do to us the next.

JIMMY (*puts down the paper, stares at* BAMJEE, *repeating, almost bored*):   We – are – black – too.

BAMJEE (*in a rage, to* MRS BAMJEE):   You encourage him! No respect. One of these loafers throwing stones, burning motorcars. Don't listen any more to their parents... 'Fatima' isn't good enough, your daughter has to paint her face and call herself 'Girlie', like a cheap white girl from the streets... Now you encourage him! Encourage him to go with black hooligans and make trouble!

JIMMY: I can think for myself! I'm the one who decides what I do. I won't lick the feet of the Boers[6] to keep a hawker's licence and a hovel like this. D'you think the whites don't spit on you?

AMINA *has come in. She looks on at the tension.*

MRS BAMJEE (*deflecting the anger of the two men, soothing*): In our family there's respect, Jimmy... He doesn't mean it, Yusuf – and you don't either, you know how well he's always done at school, he never neglects his studies...

There is a brief, bristling silence.

MRS BAMJEE: Oh I forgot what I wanted to tell you ... Girlie was here this afternoon, she says Mohammed's brother is engaged – that's nice, isn't it? His mother will be pleased; she was worried.

JIMMY: Why was she worried?

MRS BAMJEE: Well, she wanted to see him settled. There's a party on Sunday week – you'd better give me your suit to take to the cleaner's tomorrow, Yusuf.

AMINA: I'll have nothing to wear, Ma.

MRS BAMJEE *scratches her sallow face, concerned.*

MRS BAMJEE: Perhaps Girlie will lend you her pink, eh? She won't be able to get into it now. Tomorrow when she's home from work you run over to her place and say I say will she lend it to you.

Calm has been restored; her commonplaces have lulled everyone back to security within her orbit. BAMJEE *rolls his cigarette, the 'little boys' play on the floor,* JIMMY *returns to the newspaper. Her arm round her mother in feminine intimacy,* AMINA *and* MRS BAMJEE *exeunt to the kitchen.*

Scene 37
Ext. City/suburbs. Day.

BAMJEE *sees newspaper posters as he drives through streets in his lorry*: School boycotts, stonings, riots, etc.

Scene 38
Int. BAMJEE *living-room. Day.*

MRS BAMJEE *at the duplicator.*

---

[6] *Boers*: South Africans of Dutch descent.

Scene 39
Int. BAMJEE *house. Day.*

> BAMJEE *coming down passage from bedroom after afternoon nap. He carries a transistor from which loud commentary on a sports match is heard. Commentary establishes day is Saturday. He is in stockinged feet, rumpled.*

Scene 40
Int. BAMJEE *living-room. Day.*

> BAMJEE *opens living-room door on gathering of* MRS BAMJEE, MRS NDAWO *and two other* AFRICAN WOMEN, *drinking tea.* MRS BAMJEE *looks up and smiles.* BAMJEE *hurriedly closes door.*

Scene 41
Int. BAMJEE *bedroom. Day.*

> BAMJEE *lying on the bed.* MRS BAMJEE *tiptoes in, goes to wardrobe where files and papers are stored on top, and takes down a file marked 'Women's Federation'.* BAMJEE *opens his eyes.*

BAMJEE: Tea-parties with them. Not a thing other Indian women would have in their house.

> MRS BAMJEE *looks round apologetically at him, goes out with the file.*

Scene 42
Ext. Mosque. Day.

> *Façade of mosque with Gandhi's tin mosque building alongside.* BAMJEE *walking up Vorster Street to the mosque. Wealthy Indians drawing up in large cars, entering mosque with car-keys dangling: others arriving on foot.* BAMJEE *enters, disappears.*

Scene 43
Int. BAMJEE *living-room. Day.*

> *Hum of duplicator over. Duplicator working;* MRS BAMJEE's *hands.*

Scene 44
Ext. Mosque. Day.

> *Mosque tower. Hum of duplicator becomes voice of the muezzin,[7] calling the faithful to prayer.*

---

[7] *muezzin*: Muslim crier who proclaims the hour of prayer.

Scene 45

Int. BAMJEE *living-room. Night.*

Lamplight. AMINA's *bare feet and calves, where she stands on the dining table among* MRS BAMJEE's *leaflets, papers.* MRS BAMJEE *pinning the hem of a pink dress. Seen at the level of the hem,* AMINA *pirouettes slowly. C.U.* MRS BAMJEE, *pins bristling from her mouth, head drawn back, judging evenness of the hem.* JIMMY *enters, carrying a duffel coat.*

JIMMY: Ma, while you've got your sewing stuff, could you put back this button?

MRS BAMJEE (*mouth closed on pins*):   Mmm. (*Signals to him to put the coat over chair.*)

AMINA *standing on floor, hands held away from her sides, looking down at herself in the pink dress.*
C.U. MRS BAMJEE, *stacking papers in cardboard boxes, looks round to smile at the sight of* AMINA.

Scene 46

Int. BAMJEE *bedroom. Night.*

Loud knocking, which continues throughout action. BAMJEE *and* MRS BAMJEE *asleep in their bed.* BAMJEE *snores heavily. C.U.* MRS BAMJEE's *eyes wide, face very still on pillow. She slides carefully out of the bed, not waking* BAMJEE, *and leaves bedroom.*

Scene 47

Int. BAMJEE *living-room. Night.*

MRS BAMJEE *turns on light as she comes in. She wears a long nightgown; hair in a plait. Camera pans with her gaze swiftly over the room: the mantel clock showing 3 a.m., the duplicator, the boxes of papers under the table, etc. She snatches* JIMMY's *coat from the chair, struggles into it, and goes along passage to the front door in the light from the room behind her.*

Scene 48

Ext./Int. BAMJEE *passage. Night.*

P.O.V.[8] *over her shoulder, she unfastens with trembling hands the complicated locks and padlocks, etc. Knocking stops.*

TWO PLAIN-CLOTHES POLICEMEN *stand there.*

---

[8] *P.O.V.*: point of view.

WHITE POLICEMAN: Zanip Bamjee?

P.O.V. camera, he shows his police identity card.

Scene 49
Int. BAMJEE *living-room. Night.*

> *The faces of sleepy children,* AHMED, FAROUK, *peeping bewilderedly round the door. The* POLICEMEN *searching through papers, turning the room upside-down. They make brusque remarks to one another in Afrikaans. The word 'coolie-woman'[9] is heard . . .* JIMMY *in his pyjamas, stands firm behind his mother.*

JIMMY: What're you looking for? Bombs? Communists?

> *The* POLICEMEN *tell him in Afrikaans to shut up and not be cheeky, or they'll take him, too.* 'Hou jou bek, jong',[10] *etc.* MRS BAMJEE *squeezes* JIMMY'S *hand tightly to hold him back.*

MRS BAMJEE: Behind the ironing-board – there on the back stoep[11] – there's a suitcase. Bring it for me?

WHITE POLICEMAN (*examining duplicator*):   Gaan roep Van Staden – dis bleddy swaar . . .[12]

> 2ND POLICEMAN *runs out.*

WHITE POLICEMAN: What you use this thing for? Ay?

MRS BAMJEE: I'm secretary of several welfare organizations.

WHITE POLICEMAN: Welfare! So that's what you call it! (*Jeering laughter*)

Scene 50
Int. BAMJEE *bedroom. Night.*

> BAMJEE *waking up with a start, in the familiar fear of having overslept. Fumbles for alarm clock; sees 3.15 a.m. Plunges back on pillow. Becomes aware of empty place beside him; feels along bed with his hand. His eyes open; he is conscious of male voices in the house. He gets out of bed and goes to the window, pulls aside the heavy curtain and net curtain, peers through the wire burglar-proofing.*

Scene 51
Ext. BAMJEE's *street. Night.*

---

[9] *coolie-woman*: offensive term for an Indian woman.
[10] *Hou jou bek, jong*: Shut your trap, boy (Afrikaans).
[11] *stoep*: terraced veranda.
[12] *Gaan roep Van Staden – dis bleddy swaar*: Go and call Van Staden – it's bloody heavy (Afrikaans).

Under streetlight, two Volkswagens stand in the empty street. The head of a DRIVER *just discernible in one.*

Scene 52
Int. BAMJEE *living-room. Night.*

2ND POLICEMAN *and* DRIVER *picking up duplicator, cursing and bumping into furniture.* WHITE POLICEMAN *examining piles of children's comic-books, etc.* BAMJEE *stands in doorway, wearing an old shirt, barefoot. He wanders in, dazed. The* 2ND POLICEMAN *and* DRIVER *push him aside, almost crush him as they go out with the duplicator.*

MRS BAMJEE: Yusuf, it's for me.

BAMJEE *stands there, a grotesque, humiliated figure before the* WHITE POLICEMAN, *his children, the chaos of the room.*

BAMJEE (*shouting at her as if they were alone*):   There you are! That's what you've got for it. Didn't I tell you? Didn't I? That's the end of it now. That's the finish. That's what it's come to.

JIMMY *comes in from kitchen with a cardboard school-case, bearing the amateurishly painted legend:* FATIMA BAMJEE STD VI.

JIMMY: Girlie's old one, Ma…

Following action and dialogue take place at pace of confusion, P.O.V. BAMJEE, *to whom the camera keeps returning briefly where he stands ignored and helpless. Now and then the* 2ND POLICEMAN *says 'Ekskuus' as he pushes past.*

2ND POLICEMAN *and* DRIVER, *directed by* WHITE POLICEMAN, *come in and out from other parts of the house, carrying out to the cars files, newspapers, etc., an old typewriter.*

AMINA (*running in*):   I've found your clean blouse, Ma…

WHITE POLICEMAN *is paging ponderously through books:* How to Teach Yourself Accountancy, The Book of Hobbies for Boys, *battered dictionary, etc.* FAROUK *has found a packet of sweets, unearthed by the search. He sits cross-legged, hidden by the to-and-fro of adults, eating.*

JIMMY (*blowing dust out of open suitcase*):   Is it big enough?
WHITE POLICEMAN (*looks behind Gandhi portrait; calls over his shoulder to* 2ND POLICEMAN):   Vat hierdie boeke.[13] (*Picks up Jawaharlal Nehru's[14] auto-biography, to toss on to the pile of books.*)

---

[13] *Vat hierdie boeke*: Take these books (Afrikaans).
[14] *Nehru*: first prime minister of India (1950–66). He joined Gandhi's passive resistance movement in 1919 and served five and a half years in jail for his nationalist activities.

MRS BAMJEE's *hand on his arm. He wheels around as if attacked.*

MRS BAMJEE: Oh, don't take that, *please.*

WHITE POLICEMAN *holds the book up, away from her.* JIMMY *is swiftly at her side.*

JIMMY: What does it matter, Ma?
MRS BAMJEE (*to* WHITE POLICEMAN):   It's for my children.
JIMMY: Ma, leave it ... Who ever reads it, anyway...?
MRS BAMJEE: One day ... you will...
AHMED: Your slippers, Ma. (*Shakes them in front of her.*)

FARIDA *wanders in half-asleep and* AMINA *picks her up.*

WHITE POLICEMAN: Get dressed. Get your things. I give you ten minutes.

FAROUK *stealthily stuffing sweets.* MRS BAMJEE *goes out (to bedroom) with* AMINA *and* JIMMY *following.*

WHITE POLICEMAN (*looks at* BAMJEE, *sniggers*):   You not going to see your wife for a long time, Bamjee. You cook your own curry.

MRS BAMJEE *comes back wearing her usual clothes, and a shabby cloth coat. She carries the cardboard suitcase and* JIMMY's *coat; puts* JIMMY's *coat over chair. She stands with her children behind her. She turns and kisses them, one by one. She is tense, controlled, with her usual gentle smile; the police do not press her but she seems to be in a hurry to get out of this curious limelight.*

BAMJEE (P.O.V. *all others in the room; accusing wife, police, children*):   What am I going to do?
MRS BAMJEE: It'll be all right. Girlie will help. The big children can manage. And Yusuf—

The younger CHILDREN *crowd around her,* FARIDA *clings to her trouser-leg, they ask questions:* 'When are you coming back?', 'Who's going to take me to school?', *etc.*

WHITE POLICEMAN: Get a move on. Come on.
MRS BAMJEE (*above clamour of children*):   I want to speak to my husband.
WHITE POLICEMAN: But make it quick.

MRS BAMJEE *moves aside from the children.* BAMJEE *moves to her, stiff and reluctant. Faces of* POLICEMEN, *watching the couple. Faces of the* CHILDREN, *watching their parents.*
BAMJEE's *face hardening suspiciously in anticipation of being given a political message to convey.*

BAMJEE (*hoarse and low voice*):   I'm not mixed up with this business. I won't run messages.

MRS BAMJEE (*low voice, eager, hasty*):   On Sunday. Take them on Sunday.

BAMJEE *looks at her uncomprehendingly; makes a gesture: I don't know what you're talking about.*

MRS BAMJEE: The engagement party. They shouldn't miss it. Mohammed will be offended.

The sound of the cars driving away. The faces of the CHILDREN, BAMJEE, *hearing it. Silence.*

Scene 53
Int. BAMJEE's *passage. Night.*

Silence is broken by JIMMY *going to bolt and lock the front door.*

Scene 54
Int. BAMJEE *living-room. Night.*

JIMMY *looking at his father.* BAMJEE *sitting heavily in his armchair. The* CHILDREN *chatter:* 'Where'd they take Ma?' 'Will she be home when we get up tomorrow?' 'Silly – you heard what the policeman said . . .' JIMMY *sees his coat on chairback. Pauses a moment, takes coat, puts it over his pyjamas. Pauses again.*

JIMMY: Going to tell Girlie.

Scene 55
Int. CHILDREN's *rooms. Night/dawn.*

The CHILDREN *in their rooms. The policemen have scattered their toys, etc. They are over-excited, grumble; resist* AMINA's *attempts to get them back to bed.*

Scene 56
Int. BAMJEE *living-room. Night/dawn.*

BAMJEE *slumped in his chair, hearing their squabbles, crying of* FARIDA. *At last, quiet. He is alone, the night around him in the disordered room. His eyes meet the mantel clock and he sees it is not night, but an hour he should have recognized in his bones: 4.45, the time he has to get up every morning.*

Scene 57
Int. BAMJEE *bedroom. Dawn.*

BAMJEE *in the bedroom: papers and clothes, contents of drawers, spilled by the police search. The empty double bed. He is pulling on trousers, dirty white hawker's coat; winds the grey muffler round his neck up to unshaven chin.*

Scene 58
Ext. BAMJEE *street. Early morning.*

Sound of lorry starting, revving the engine, over. Sun up, striking obliquely down the street. Wind blowing trees, paper.

Scene 59
Int. BAMJEE *living-room. Evening.*

Empty space on sideboard where duplicator used to be. The Taj Mahal, wedding photograph, etc., have not been put back in place. The pot-plants with their ribbon bows, wilting, unwatered. BAMJEE *in his chair, alone.*

Scene 60
Int. CHILDREN's *rooms. Evening.*

AHMED, FAROUK, FARIDA *jumping from bed to bed, a fierce clandestine game behind the shut door in their room.*

Scene 61
Int. Bathroom. Evening.

AHMED *and* FAROUK *playing in the bath. Water splashing everywhere.*

Scene 62
Int. BAMJEE *living-room. Evening.*

AMINA *and* JIMMY *silently doing schoolwork on dining table.*
JIMMY *looking at his father, seated in the usual chair. C.U.* JIMMY *seems about to speak. Closed face of* BAMJEE. AMINA, *nervous, looking at her father imploringly.*

Scene 63
Int. School classroom. Day.

JIMMY *addressing student protest meeting. He half-sits, half-stands, hitched against a teacher's table, with two other student leaders, a coloured girl and Indian boy.*

JIMMY: What is 'coloured'?[15] What is 'Asian'? We won't sell black unity for a few handouts offered because the government wants to divide us by classifying us 'coloured' or 'Asian'. We don't recognize this place 'South Africa' with its racist words and laws ... (*Applause*) We are going to support our brothers and sisters. We want the same education for every-body, the same education as whites. When we finish school, we want to hold down the same jobs as whites. (*Applause*) Tomorrow we are going to march full-strength to Westbury to support our brothers and sisters, and we are not scared of what we meet ... (*Shouts:* 'Freedom' ... 'Down with Bantu Education')[16] Many of our brothers and sisters are in jail. *My mother is in jail.* I am ready to join them ... (*Shouts:* 'Azania!'[17] 'Amandla!'[18] 'Freedom!')

Scene 64
Int. BAMJEE *living-room. Evening.*

BAMJEE *family eating.* AMINA *has cooked. She anxiously brings food to and fro between living-room and kitchen.* JIMMY *helps; coaxes* FARIDA *to eat.*

FAROUK: It's not nice. I don't like it.

GIRLIE *and her husband* MOHAMMED *enter through the kitchen.*

GIRLIE: Have you found out?
BAMJEE (*surly*):   What?
GIRLIE: Where they've taken her?
BAMJEE (*bursts out; a dam of resentment breaking*):   What have we done that your mother leaves us like this? Does she care what happens to her husband and children? The blacks, the blacks ... that's all she knows ...

MOHAMMED *is sampling one of the dishes. He masticates serenely, look-ing from one to the other – his wife and her father – in their state of emotion.*

---

[15] *coloured:* of mixed racial descent.
[16] *Bantu Education:* 'The segregated educational system and syllabuses for blacks, devised by the South African government on a lower standard than that provided for whites. "Bantu", from the Zulu word for "people" (*abantu*), was for many years the official government term for blacks, and the usage lingers although the term has been discredited as meaningless.' (Author's note)
[17] *Azania!:* 'Adopted at various times by different black liberation movements as the name by which the future South Africa, when free of white minority rule, will be called.' (Author's note)
[18] *Amandla!:* 'Zulu: Power. Widely used by black (and some non-racial) liberation movements as a dedicatory avowal. Called by a speaker, it brings its corresponding response from any gather-ing, "*Awethu!*": To the people!' (Author's note)

Scene 65
Int. BAMJEE *kitchen. Evening.*

> GIRLIE *and* AMINA *washing up.* JIMMY *leans tensely against wall/cupboard, arms folded and shoulders hunched.*

JIMMY: If he won't do anything, we will. You'll take off work tomorrow.
GIRLIE: And your school?
JIMMY: We've decided to boycott in solidarity with Soweto and Westbury, anyway.

Scene 66
Ext. City. Day.

> JIMMY *and* GIRLIE *at bus-stop for Lenasia.*

Scene 67
Ext. Lenasia. Day.

> JIMMY *and* GIRLIE *getting off bus in Lenasia.*

Scene 68
Ext. Lenasia. DR KHAN's *house. Day.*

> JIMMY *opening gate on which is well-polished brass plate:* DR ABDUL KHAN MB.CHB (WITS),[19] MD (EDINBURGH). *Camera pulls back on fine, upper-middle-class Lenasia house.*

Scene 69
Int. DR KHAN's *living-room. Day.*

> GIRLIE's *bare toes, in sandals, wiggling a little in thick pile of a shaggy carpet.* JIMMY *and* GIRLIE *seated with* DR KHAN. GIRLIE's *eyes go round the room, with its contemporary lamps, pictures, Kalil Gibran[20] illuminated text, hi-fi equipment.* JIMMY *does not notice his surroundings.*

DR KHAN: She's been moved to Naboomspruit. We've briefed Asvat as her legal representative; they couldn't refuse to reveal her whereabouts to him ...
GIRLIE: Naboomspruit ... Is it far?
DR KHAN (*a gesture towards* JIMMY):   An hour and a half's drive, I suppose? –

---

[19] *MB.ChB (Wits)*: Bachelor of Medicine, Bachelor of Surgery (Witwatersrand University).
[20] *Kalil Gibran*: Syrian poet and painter (1883–1931).

Asvat says they've put five or six women politicals there, whites too. But apparently the accommodation's rather better than in Pretoria prison.

JIMMY: Did the lawyer see my mother?

DR KHAN: Not yet ... he'll arrange permission for a family visit.

GIRLIE: They sent her so far away ...

JIMMY: When can we go?

DR KHAN: Only one member of the family ... and I don't think it should be you, Jimmy. Someone in the student movement ... First of all, I don't think the police would grant you permission to see her and, secondly, I don't think it's too healthy for you to ask ...

GIRLIE: Dr Khan, you know my father couldn't go, he is out with ... his business every day ... (*she dries up, embarrassed*). How do I get the permit?

JIMMY: I should see my mother.

DR KHAN (*shakes his head*): You are like your mother. You'll put your responsibilities to the Movement first. (*To* GIRLIE) Don't worry about the permit, Asvat will fix it for you.

Scene 70
Int. BAMJEE *bedroom. Day.*

BAMJEE, *unshaven, winding muffler round his neck.*

Scene 71
Ext. Diagonal street/market. Day.

Vegetables being loaded on BAMJEE'S *lorry.*

Scene 72
Ext. White suburban street. Day.

The lorry in white suburbs. BAMJEE *sees newspaper posters referring to continued unrest in schools, etc., in black and coloured townships.*

BAMJEE *weighing onions for* AFRIKAANS WOMAN (*Scene 18*). *She stands by with basket, her hair in curlers under scarf.*

AFRIKAANS WOMAN: Ag, don't you want a bargain? I'm selling my old freezer. It's good like new, only my husband's buying me a bigger one. I give it to you cheap, man. A real bargain. Thirty rands[21] – cash. You can put it on the lorry and take it home to your wife now.

BAMJEE (*sending the onions rolling into her basket*): I have no wife.

---

[21] *rands*: South African currency.

Scene 73

Int. BAMJEE *living-room. Day.*

> BAMJEE *in his chair.* JIMMY *stands in front of him.*

JIMMY: Girlie needs money for the train ticket to Naboomspruit.

> BAMJEE *broods a moment in silence.*

BAMJEE: How much?

JIMMY (*equally shortly*):   Twelve rands eighty return.

> *A pause in which it seems* BAMJEE *will refuse. Then he stands up, puts his hand in his trouser pocket, sorts from handful of coins and small-denomination notes a ten-rand one and puts it on the table. Out of the pocket in his hawker's coat, lying there, he takes a worn wallet, and extracts from one of the folds a five-rand note.*
> *Five-rand note in his hand; hesitation.*
> JIMMY *watches the hand.*
> *The hand puts the five-rand note back in the wallet and puts another ten-rand one on the table.*
> JIMMY *makes to pick up the money. Pauses and looks up under his brows at his father.*

JIMMY: It's only twelve rands eighty for the ticket.

> BAMJEE *looks stony.*
> JIMMY *looks at* BAMJEE *keenly.*
> BAMJEE *does not respond.*
> JIMMY *picks up the money.*

Scene 74

Ext. Oriental plaza. Day.

> GIRLIE's *hands, feeling cardigan at stall.*

SHOPKEEPER: Take this one. Sale price.

> *Camera pulls back to* GIRLIE.

GIRLIE: Not warm enough. It's cold where the lady is.

> *Plastic bag with trade-name into which another cardigan is being dropped.*

Scene 75

Ext. Diagonal street/market. Day.

> BAMJEE *talking to* ELDERLY INDIAN *while produce is loaded by* MOSES.

BAMJEE: Ah, yes, yes, you can see how I am – eh – you see what has been done to me. Five children at home, and I am on the road all day. I come to the house seven, eight o'clock. No woman there, nothing. What are you to do?

ELDERLY INDIAN (*he has been folding betel leaf*[22] *while listening to* BAMJEE; *he puts it in his mouth and chews while he speaks*): If it is God's will, what can you do? If God wills . . .

BAMJEE: I never had a wife like other men. And what about her children . . . when the police were there, taking her away like a criminal . . . my wife! . . . the children were all running around, she was running around, a family occasion. Just like weddings and engagements, I don't know what, she always makes such a fuss and preparation . . . To put me in this mess . . .

Scene 76
Ext. School yard/street. Day.

JIMMY *carrying home-painted banner with other students:* SCRAP GHETTO EDUCATION.

Scene 77
Int. BAMJEE *kitchen. Day.*

AMINA *ironing* BAMJEE's *hawker's coat.*

Scene 78
Ext. Fordsburg/Pageview. Day.

AHMED, FAROUK *and* FARIDA *playing hide-and-seek in ruined shops, dodging round bulldozers.*

Scene 79[23]

Int. BAMJEE *living-room. Day.*

BAMJEE *and* TWO NEIGHBOURS; *they carry offerings of food. The three sit as if in a house of mourning.* 1ST NEIGHBOUR (*a fat woman with low-cut choli (blouse), jewellery and painted toenails, a red spot painted on her forehead*): A cake for the children. (*Putting on the table a plate covered with an embroidered cloth.*)

---

[22] *betel leaf*: leaf of evergreen plant chewed in the East.
[23] This scene was cut from the completed film.

Moody glance of acknowledgement from BAMJEE. *He shakes his head slowly, lifts a limp hand in helplessness.*

BAMJEE: Five children in the house, I am on the lorry all day . . .

2ND NEIGHBOUR (*wearing trousers and tunic, well groomed, both modest and gushing*):   Mutton curry and some fresh roti.[24] Just made this morning.

She carefully slides on to the table a plastic container; holds her breath, as if in delicate consideration for the presence of a corpse.

BAMJEE: . . . well, you see for yourself how I am. They walk in here in the middle of the night and leave a houseful of children . . . I'm out on the lorry all day, I have to earn a living . . .

The breasts of the 1ST NEIGHBOUR *heave with emotion above the neckline of her choli, under the gauze of the sari.*

1ST NEIGHBOUR: Poor Mrs Bamjee . . . such a kind lady . . .

Scene 80
Ext. Country station. Day.

GIRLIE *descending from train on country-town station. She sets off up the street carrying the plastic bag with trade-name (Scene 74). She stops a black woman who is carrying parcels on her head.*

GIRLIE: Do you know where is the prison?

BLACK WOMAN *gives exclamation; says something in her own language.*

GIRLIE (*tries Afrikaans*):   Sê vir my, asseblief, waar is die gevangenis?[25]

Scene 81
Int. BAMJEE *living-room. Day.*

AMINA *serving cold drinks to the* TWO NEIGHBOURS. *She is silent, polite, never looks at her father.*

Scene 82
Int. BAMJEE *living-room. Day.*

AMINA, JIMMY, AHMED, FAROUK, FARIDA *gathered round* GIRLIE, *dressed as in Scene 80.* BAMJEE *greedily drinking tea at table.*

---

[24] *roti*: Indian savoury stuffed pancake.
[25] *Sê vir my, asseblief, waar is die gevangenis?*: Please tell me, where is the prison? (Afrikaans).

GIRLIE: She's all right. They don't let her have books – you know, she's alone and that ... but she's okay. She speaks quite ordinary ... and everything. They're allowed to knit, she said I should bring some wool, they'll take that in for her. And soap ... Of course I couldn't ask too much – the police are right there next to you in the room – she said tell Jimmy she was 'talking a long time the first week'. I don't know what she meant ...

JIMMY: Interrogation. Did she stand up all right – she wasn't weak?

GIRLIE: No, man, I told you, she's okay.

JIMMY: Did she say anything about sleep?

GIRLIE: Well, Ma, you know – like always, Ma always looks a bit tired. She's okay.

JIMMY: That's torture ... they've kept her from sleeping, 'Talking a lot' ..., kept her awake for days and nights, questioning her ... that's torture.

BAMJEE *suddenly puts down cup and walks out of the room, the* OTHERS *fall silent.*

AMINA: Oh, Jimmy, you know horrible things.

Scene 83
Int. Shop. Day.

BAMJEE *complaining to* SHOPKEEPER *at corner general store.* BAMJEE *has loaf of bread under his arm.*

BAMJEE: I don't understand it. Why it must happen to me? A good mother ... not one of those modern women who cut their hair and wear European skirts up to here. But this madness ... and the blacks, what they will do to us if they get power ... I say to her, you'll see what they do ... murder, burn ...

Scene 84
Ext. Fordsburg Street. Day.

AHMED *with schoolbag on his back, crying as he walks home from school. He stops and buys an ice-cream from cart attended by* BLACK VENDOR. *He licks the cone and tears mingle with the ice-cream.*

BLACK VENDOR (*laughing*): What is the matter? You been naughty at school?

Scene 85
Int. BAMJEE *living-room. Day.*

BAMJEE *enters, home from work, in his hawker's coat. All the* CHILDREN *are gathered round* AHMED. JIMMY *is paging through violent comic-book, but paying attention to action.*

FAROUK (*rushing up to his father, importantly*):   They've been cruel to Ahmed!

BAMJEE (*dull and stern*):   What has he done?

FAROUK: Nothing! Nothing! Ahmed didn't do nothing!

AMINA: They did it at school today. They made an example of him.

BAMJEE (*impatient gesture*):   What is an example?

AMINA (*gabbling, indignant*):   The teacher made him come up and stand in front of the whole class, and he told them, 'You see this boy? His mother's in jail because she likes the blacks so much. She wants the Indians to be the same as blacks who live in mud houses in Zululand.'

BAMJEE: It's terrible. (*His hands fall away to his sides.*) Did she ever think of this?

JIMMY: That's why Ma's in *there*. (*He tosses comic-book aside.*) That's all the kids need to know. Ma's in there because things like this happen. Petersen's a coloured teacher, and it's his black blood that's brought him trouble all his life. He hates anyone who says everybody's the same because that takes away from him his bit of whiteness. What d'you expect? A poor brain-washed idiot! It's nothing to make too much fuss about.

BAMJEE (*mumbling*):   Of course, you are fifteen and you know everything.

JIMMY: I don't say that. But I know Ma, anyway. (*He laughs confidently.*)

Scene 86

Int. BAMJEE *kitchen. Day.*

FARIDA *singing to herself, a nursery rhyme learned at school.* AMINA *at the stove, cooking, very responsible.* GIRLIE *chopping vegetables.* FAROUK *and* AHMED *making a model cut out from cereal box. A knock at the kitchen door.* GIRLIE *gets up, wipes her hands on her belly, opens door.* MRS NDAWO *in doorway.*

MRS NDAWO: Is your father here?

AMINA *looking round from her pots.*

GIRLIE: Only us. He does come home at lunchtime Saturdays, but he's not here yet. But please, come in.

MRS NDAWO: I'm your mother's friend ... the Parents' Committee.

AMINA: Oh, yes, I've seen you when you were here with my mother many times, Mrs Ndawo.

MRS NDAWO: I just wanted to tell your father ... there's a hunger strike in prison, the women at Naboomspruit are refusing food.

FAROUK (*to* AMINA):   If the food's horrible, like you cook, I don't blame them.

AMINA *frowns vehemently at him, distracted.* JIMMY *enters, adult and politically aware.*

JIMMY: What's happened?

GIRLIE: Ma won't eat anything. There's a hunger strike.

MRS NDAWO (*makes sympathetic African exclamations*):   Really, our hearts are with those women ...

JIMMY: What's the issue? What happened there?

MRS NDAWO: Charge or release. They say either they must be brought to court or they must be let go ... some have been there more than three months now.

JIMMY (*nods solidarity, proudly*):   That's it. And you're going to have a back-up campaign to support the strike?

MRS NDAWO: Those of us that are still left outside ... of course. Until they take us, too, we won't keep quiet ...

Scene 87

Ext. BAMJEE *yard. Day.*

> BAMJEE's *lorry driving into the yard.* JIMMY *coming out of house into yard. He and his father greet each other with nods, and* JIMMY *begins to help him clean out lorry, for the weekend.*

JIMMY: Ma's not eating. A hunger strike.

BAMJEE (*a face of fear and dismay*):   Another madness! I don't want to hear about it. If she wants to starve herself she must starve!

Scene 88

Int. AMINA's *bedroom. Night.*

> AMINA *sits up in the bed she shares with the sleeping* FARIDA, *doing her homework. Her eyes are puffy with crying, her nose still runs intermittently.* JIMMY *stands with his back to her, thrusting his fingers into the wire burglar screen at the window. He turns, looks at her a moment.*

JIMMY (*defiant, full of bravado and platitudes*):   He's ignorant. A victim of the system. A slave, counting his potatoes. I pity him. We have to re-educate people like that.

Scene 89

Ext. Fordsburg Street. Day.

> GIRLIE *walking past Indian stores, among shoppers. She is stopped by a pretty* YOUNG INDIAN WOMAN *carrying a* BABY *dressed up like a doll.*

YOUNG INDIAN WOMAN: Girlie – how's your mother? I only heard yesterday...?

GIRLIE: I've just been to see her.

YOUNG INDIAN WOMAN (*curious*):   Is it really true they're not eating anything?

GIRLIE (*quietly*):   The hunger strike's been on a week now.

YOUNG INDIAN WOMAN: Oh, shame, ay... (*Change of tone; looking with intimate femininity at* GIRLIE's *belly*):   How many months are you gone?

Scene 90

Ext. BAMJEE's *street. Same day.*

GIRLIE *coming up the street.* AHMED, FAROUK, FARIDA *playing in street, run to her, crowd round.*

AHMED: Did you see Ma?

FAROUK: Can she talk?

FARIDA: Did you tell her I got a gold star at school?

Scene 91

Int. BAMJEE *living-room. Same day.*

GIRLIE, JIMMY, AMINA *and other children.* GIRLIE *breathes exhaustedly, sits with her legs spread, at the table.*

GIRLIE: I feel funny sometimes, now. (*She presses her hand on her belly.*)

AMINA *runs out to kitchen.*

JIMMY: So. How was she?

GIRLIE *gestures away from herself. There is a moment of silence between them. She takes a deep breath, exhales jerkily.*

GIRLIE: All right.

JIMMY: Does she look ...?

GIRLIE: She says they take glucose and water.

JIMMY: You can live on that.

GIRLIE: She ... her face (GIRLIE *draws in her cheeks and strokes down them with both hands*).

AHMED: How long can you stay alive without eating?

JIMMY: Oh ... I don't know ... quite a long time ... if you have plenty to drink. Gandhi fasted for weeks. Months. Ma told me once.

AMINA *has come in carefully carrying a glass of milk balanced on a saucer. She gives it to* GIRLIE.

AMINA: Yes, but he nearly died. The British tried to force-feed him in prison to stop him dying. Ma told me about that too.

AHMED (*fearfully*):   Ma really hasn't had anything for a whole week? No breakfast, no supper?

GIRLIE *makes an attempt to smile, slowly shaking her head. They are all looking at her, as if to reach the reality of their mother's state through her. Her huge belly rests heavily on her thighs.*
FAROUK *slowly approaches her.*
C.U. FAROUK's *face, wondering, fascinated.*
C.U. GIRLIE's *belly, a mysterious mound under her cheap dress.*
C.U. FAROUK's *face.*
FAROUK's *hand points towards the belly, timid but irresistibly drawn.*

FAROUK: What does it eat – in there?

AHMED, FARIDA, AMINA, *giggling.*

Scene 92

Int. BAMJEE *living-room. Evening.*

The BAMJEE FAMILY *at table, without* GIRLIE. *All heads down silently over plates.* BAMJEE *stretches across table to help himself, wolfs his food, the* CHILDREN *glance at him sideways.* AHMED *pushes his food, uneaten, around his plate.* BAMJEE *dumps helping of salad on* AHMED's *plate.* AHMED's *head bows.* BAMJEE *gestures: Eat that.* AHMED *bursts into tears.* BAMJEE *pushes his own plate away in rage.*

Scene 93

Ext. City/suburb streets. Day.

BAMJEE *on his rounds with his lorry. Alone in the rattling cab he says aloud things he hears as if spoken by someone else.*

BAMJEE: A crowd of blacks who'll smash Indian shops and kill us in our houses when their time comes . . . She'll die there . . . Blacks who will burn and kill us . . .

BAMJEE *driving into yard.*

BAMJEE (*V.O.*):   For what? For what? She'll die there . . . Who'll care about her children – who, I want to ask that . . .

Scene 94

Int. BAMJEE *living-room. Evening.*

BAMJEE *walking through assembled children, without acknowledging their presence.*

BAMJEE (*V.O.*):   A mob that'll burn and kill us . . . Starve to death for *them* . . .

Scene 95
Int. BAMJEE *bedroom. Night.*

> BAMJEE *falls on the bed fully dressed, in his hawker's coat.*

BAMJEE (*V.O.*):   The lorry all day, struggling for a living, morning to night... come home to what?

> BAMJEE *sleeps as if felled by a blow.*

Scene 96
Int. BAMJEE *bedroom. Dawn.*

> BAMJEE *dragging himself up in the morning. Staggering into his trousers. Alarm clock shows 4.45 a.m.*

BAMJEE (*V.O.*):   Not a woman who paints and cuts her hair. Why must I suffer? She'll die there.
What for?
What for?

Scene 97
Ext. Mosque. Day.

> BAMJEE *is stopped by* DR KHAN *as both approach mosque for midday prayers on Friday.* DR KHAN *is elegantly dressed;* BAMJEE *unshaven and shabby, tieless as usual. Both wear the small round Muslim cap on the back of their head.*

DR KHAN: Mr Bamjee, Asvat has arranged for the women to be under medical supervision. We insisted on that – he saw the Director of Prisons. They are being carefully watched – you can be assured—

> BAMJEE *looks trapped, humiliated, held against his will by the authority and assurance of an important man in the Muslim community. He turns away angrily from* DR KHAN.

Scene 98
Int./Ext. BAMJEE *passage. Day.*

> BAMJEE *opening front door to reveal* MRS NDAWO. *She smiles and greets him. He half-closes door to keep her out.*

BAMJEE: My wife isn't here, *you* know that. Don't come to this house. Leave my children alone.

> BAMJEE *closes door on her.*

Scene 99

Ext. White suburban street. Day.

BAMJEE *serving* WHITE CUSTOMER. *She watches him closely, with unpleasant air of triumphant suspicion.*

WHITE CUSTOMER (*nagging South African voice*):   Are you sure they fresh? Every time I send my kitchen girl, you give her rubbish ...

Scene 100

Ext. City street. Day.

BAMJEE *driving his lorry.*

BAMJEE (*V.O.*):   ... morning to night ... What for? Starve there ... What for?

Scene 101

Int. BAMJEE *kitchen. Evening.*

BAMJEE *at home, silent in presence of* CHILDREN. *He slams fruit and vegetables down on table.*

Scene 102

Int. BAMJEE *bedroom. Dawn.*

BAMJEE *getting up, pulling on usual clothes.*

Scene 103

Int. BAMJEE *kitchen. Early morning.*

BAMJEE *heating up last night's brew of tea in an enamel mug. He sits wearily, already wearing his muffler, at kitchen table, drinking tea and wolfing dry bread. He keeps looking resentfully at the familiar places where his wife should be: in front of the stove, at the ironing-board left standing by* AMINA, *etc. Camera holds on plants on window-sill, now dead.*
A soft knock. GIRLIE's *freshly curled head at the window.*
BAMJEE *goes over to the door and opens it.*
GIRLIE, *heavily pregnant but neat and made-up to go to work, comes in.*
BAMJEE's *P.O.V.: her cocky smile, immodest as a white girl's, her short skirt and painted fingernails.*

BAMJEE (*desperately alarmed*):   What's the matter?
GIRLIE (*smiling*):   Don't you know? I told Mohammed he must get me up in time to catch you this morning. I wanted to be sure you wouldn't be on the lorry already.

BAMJEE (*sits down again, takes up bread and tears off a piece, dips it in tea*):   I don't know what you're talking about.

GIRLIE *comes over and puts her arm around his neck, bending to kiss the grey bristles at the side of his mouth.*

GIRLIE: Many happy returns, Bajie! Don't you know it's your birthday?
BAMJEE (*listlessly*):   No. I didn't think . . . (*shrugs off something of no importance*).

A pause, which he breaks by swiftly picking up the bread and giving his attention to eating and drinking. He swallows a piece of bread with difficulty, as if it tears his throat as it goes down.

BAMJEE: I don't remember these things.
GIRLIE (*animatedly*):   First thing she told me when I saw her yesterday – don't forget it's Bajie's birthday tomorrow. Sixty-two, sixteenth August.
BAMJEE (*eating, shrugs*):   Birthday. Something for children. Fine birthday . . . But that's how she is (*complaining*). Whether it's one of the old cousins or the neighbour's grandmother, she always knows when the birthday is. What importance my birthday, while she's sitting there in a prison? I don't understand how she can do the terrible things she does when her head is always full of woman's nonsense the same time – that's what I don't understand with her.
GIRLIE: Oh, but don't you see? It's just that. It's because she doesn't want anybody to be left out. You know? It's because she always remembers; remembers everything – people without somewhere to live, hungry kids, boys who can't get educated – remembers all the time. That's how Ma is.
BAMJEE (*complaining*):   Nobody else is like that.
GIRLIE (*looking at him deeply*):   No, nobody else. (*She looks at him, pauses. Shyly offers . . .*) And I've got a present for you: Ma's eating again. The strike's been called off.

She sits down at the table, resting her belly. BAMJEE *puts his head in his hands.* GIRLIE *looks at him.*

BAMJEE: I'm getting old . . .

BAMJEE *looks at his daughter, her face and whole body. Slowly there comes to his face a curious expression of wonder, at the fact – before him – of the burgeoning persistence of renewal.*
GIRLIE *takes his gaze with dignity. All her 'white girl' cockiness disappears.*
Very slowly, GIRLIE *leans forward, takes her father's hand and puts it against her belly.*

GIRLIE: Feel. It's alive . . .

Scene 104
Ext. City. Day.

BAMJEE *shaved and dressed in his only suit, old-fashioned brown pin-stripe, clean shirt but no tie. He looks like a peasant widower going courting. He has a small paper carrier of fruit. He is buying flowers from a stall near the city hall. He bargains with the Indian vendor over the price. The* VENDOR *lifts, dripping, from a tin of water, a large bunch of red carnations.*

VENDOR: Take these – very fresh – ruby red, look at that colour...

BAMJEE's *P.O.V.: red carnations held out to* BAMJEE.

Scene 105
Ext. Railway station. Day.

BAMJEE *on platform marked* NON-EUROPEANS. *He holds red carnations wrapped in a newspaper cone, and carrier of fruit.*

BAMJEE *boards train and fusses, arranging self and packages. He sits opposite a well-dressed Indian with briefcase.*

BAMJEE's *profile against landscape he is watching pass before window of moving train: the veld,*[26] *etc.*

WELL-DRESSED INDIAN *drums his fingers impatiently on his briefcase and looks about with a superior air, ignoring landscape.*

WELL-DRESSED INDIAN: Don't know how many years since I was in a train! My car broke down this morning. As I was leaving my house! Trouble ... always trouble ... life is always trouble ... Just today, when I have to get up to Naboomspruit ... My brother-in-law is being evicted from his shop. Same thing everywhere. But you got to know who to deal with, how to go about things – you know? I myself was told three years ago I got to get out of my place in Hillbrow and my second shop in Jeppe – men's outfitters, high-class business. You have to know how to handle things – no good to panic. There was this government chappie in Pretoria, I knew him a long time ... it cost me three thousand rands, but all right, I'm still in business, eh? Unfortunately, my brother-in-law – he's not a man of the world ... these people in small towns, you know how they are ... So of course they call me ... Are you in business?

BAMJEE: Fresh produce.

WELL-DRESSED INDIAN: Wholesale?

BAMJEE: No, I go around ...

WELL-DRESSED INDIAN: Well, I can see your visit at least doesn't mean trouble *(gestures to flowers)* – beautiful!

---

[26] *veld*: open countryside.

BAMJEE's *hands, curled, palm up, on his knees, jogged helplessly by motion of the train.*

Scene 106
Ext. Country town. Day.

BAMJEE's *back, in small town street where* GIRLIE *was seen (Scene 80), trudging, looking at same street signs.*

Scene 107
Int. Visitors' room. Prison. Day.

BAMJEE *before wire grille, flowers and fruit clutched in his hands.*

MRS BAMJEE *on other side of grille; shadowy figures of two* WARDRESSES *in background – they are presences, never brought into focus.*

MRS BAMJEE *is looking at* BAMJEE *with shy amazement, like a young girl suddenly noticed by a man she has watched from afar for a long time. Her eyes take in the newly shaven face, suit, etc. They have already exchanged through the grille the awkward period of greeting; she smiles at him slowly, after a moment of silence.*

MRS BAMJEE: When I saw it was you . . . I thought Girlie must have had the baby . . .

BAMJEE *shakes his head.*

MRS BAMJEE: We're only supposed to talk about family matters. Jimmy's all right? I don't know whether I can believe Girlie . . . He's not . . . where I am? I believe there are some young ones . . . also inside . . . (*she glances back at listening* WARDRESSES).

BAMJEE: He's all right. Runs the whole house, the children.

MRS BAMJEE (*smiling, quoting*):   He's fifteen and he knows everything.

Silence from BAMJEE. *He gazes at her.*
C.U. MRS BAMJEE's *face patterned over by the wire grille.*

MRS BAMJEE: It's always hard . . . there are so many things to talk about and with people listening . . . you're always thinking time's going to be up in a minute . . . before you know where to begin . . . (*hurriedly, change of tone*). You'll remember to pay the light and water account – where did I put it? – oh, yes, it's usually under that fancy cigarette box Auntie Zubi gave us, you know, between Girlie's wedding picture and the Taj Mahal. If they didn't take it away with the other stuff that night. The house must have looked a mess . . . – But make sure, because imagine if the water and light's cut off . . . the children . . .

BAMJEE *nods in acceptance of instructions.*

MRS BAMJEE: And ... you ... are you all right?

BAMJEE *nods slowly.*

MRS BAMJEE: Yusuf, I'm sorry ... you have to think about all these (*a gesture of the hands, opening out*) ... while I sit here ... (*change of tone: matter-of-fact, cheerful*) Maybe I'll be home in time to go and pay, myself.

BAMJEE: A wonderful woman.

MRS BAMJEE: What?

BAMJEE: Dr Khan said.

MRS BAMJEE: When did you speak to him?

BAMJEE: Not now. Long ago. He was coming out of the house.

MRS BAMJEE (*embarrassed, smiling, shrugs*):   He has to be encouraging – you know – a way of speaking.

BAMJEE *awkwardly shows carrier of fruit. He takes out a pear.*

BAMJEE: They won't take these in. The best pears – just coming into season, first time this week. And some nice carnations.

He lifts bouquet, in its newspaper, towards the grille.
Shadowy figures of WARDRESSES *moving forward.*

WARDRESS'S VOICE: Keep back. You are not allowed to make contact with the prisoner.

BAMJEE'S *hand holding up the red carnations. Against the grille, they fill frame.*
MRS BAMJEE'S *face above, among the red carnations, behind the grille.*

MRS BAMJEE: Yusuf, I can smell the scent from here.

SUGGESTIONS FOR WRITING AND DISCUSSION

1 What do you learn from this play about life in South Africa?
2 Describe the attitudes of the other characters to Mrs Bamjee's involvement in political activity.
3 Write an account of the character of Mrs Bamjee.
4 Describe the relationship between Mrs Bamjee and her husband.
5 Who do you think is the central character in the play – Mrs Bamjee or her husband? Justify your answer.
6 Describe the kind of family life the Bamjees live.
7 Comment on the different racial attitudes revealed in the play.
8 Justify the view that this is not only a play about life in South Africa today, but is also relevant to other societies.
9 What do you think the author is trying to say in this play about personal courage, and why did she choose the medium of television to say it?
10 Why do you think this play has been banned in South Africa? What are

your views on this decision?

11 *Nadine Gordimer originally wrote* A Chip of Glass Ruby *as a short story. What do you think is gained by turning it into a television play?*

12 *Choose two scenes from the play that work particularly well in televisual terms and explain why.*

13 *Write about your own views and feelings on apartheid.*

14 *Imagine you are Jimmy or Girlie. Write about your views of your family and the political and social situation you are in.*

15 *Write a short account of the position of Indians (with regard to, for instance, the vote, work, freedom of movement, education) in South Africa at the present time.*

16 *Mrs Bamjee mentions Gandhi in the play. Find out what you can about Gandhi's activities in South Africa and give a talk about 'Gandhi in South Africa', or write it up as a report.*

17 *A much-used sports field near where you live is in danger of being sold off by the local council to developers for houses or offices and car parks. Outline a plan of action to mount a campaign to prevent this happening.*

18 *Improvise or write your own script or short story about a woman who is very involved in political activities and whose husband is very against this.*

19 *Mrs Bamjee goes on hunger strike because she is being held without a charge being laid. Investigate what the law is in this country with regard to holding people without charge.*

20 *'A crowd of blacks ...' (p. 129). What is Mr Bamjee's attitude (at this point) to what is happening? Are you sympathetic or unsympathetic towards him? Why?*

21 *Outline how Mr Bamjee has changed by the end of the play.*

22 *Write your own version of the next episode after the 'end' of the play.*

23 *Write a script or short story about a family where a member of the family is in jail.*

24 *Has this play changed your attitude to South Africa at all? If so, in what way?*